If you have always thought that ready theology was a dull and bland exercise, you're in for a surprise. *Common Grounds* is an engrossing and fun book. It is also a book that expresses the eternal verities of the Christian faith with great freshness, insight, and clarity. If you're a believer, you'll rejoice once again in the truth you have come to love and, if you aren't a believer, this book will make you think. And, who knows? It may even cause you to reconsider some stereotypes about Christians and the Christian faith that are well . . . stereotypes. Read this book. You'll be glad you did.

—Steve Brown—
Professor of Preaching at Reformed Theological Seminary–Orlando
Teacher of the nationally syndicated radio program, *Key Life*

I found myself eagerly anticipating those coffeehouse conversations. This book is a fresh approach to knowing God and provides an excellent model for engaging our culture with grace and truth. I highly recommend it to you.

—Mark Gauthier—
National Director, Campus Ministry
Campus Crusade for Christ

Postmodern America is a playground of worldviews and lifestyles. Christians are learning new ways of presenting the case for the authentic gospel of Jesus Christ in this postmodern context. *Common Grounds* represents one of those new ways of telling the story and making the case. Ben Young and Glenne Lucke serve on the front lines of today's ministry. Their new book is driven by a compelling narrative and an even more compelling argument. If you want to reach the postmodern generation, read this book and give it to your friends.

—R. Albert Mohler Jr., President—
The Southern Baptist Theological Seminary

Common Grounds represents the Christian faith as an intellectual double shot of espresso, serving it with uncommon candor and refreshingly relevant insight. Ben Young and Glenn Lucke have provided an incredible tool for believers to provide a ready defense of their faith, and they raise critical questions too substantial for the allegedly objective to ignore.

—Mac Richard, Pastor—
Lake Hills Church
Austin, Texas

Common Grounds is a winsome and delightful exploration of anxieties, big questions, and the path of life and hope among young friends in an emerging generation. The writing brings a fresh and intelligent voice to questions of what matters and why. Glenn Lucke and Ben Young honor these questions with a story of spiritual insight and cultural sophistication . . . that is just fun to read.

—Kelly Monroe—
Editor and coauthor of *Finding God at Harvard*
Founder of *The Veritas Forum*

At last, a story that explores the questions so many of us have about faith. An exciting and practical read for both believers and skeptics.

—Dr. Richard L. Pratt Jr.—
Professor of Old Testament, Reformed Theological Seminary–Orlando
Third Millennium Ministries, President

In this book, (and in volume two, which I hope to see soon) Glenn Lucke and Ben Young have wisely taken up the ancient form of "dialogue" to introduce students who are at the beginning of their intellectual journey to the marriage of theology and life. It is a book that is generous in tone, confessional in structure, and pastorally attentive to the questions that students actually ask.

—Greg Thompson—
Reformed University Fellowship
University of Virginia

Common Grounds

Common Grounds

Ben Young
Glenn Lucke

CONVERSATIONS ABOUT THE THINGS THAT MATTER MOST

BROADMAN
& HOLMAN
PUBLISHERS

Nashville, Tennesse

0-8054-2697-3

Published by Broadman & Holman Publishers,
Nashville, Tennessee

Dewey Decimal Classification: 231.5
Subject Heading: GOD—WILL

All Scripture citation is from the NIV, the Holy Bible,
New International Version, copyright © 1973, 1978,
1984 by International Bible Society.

1 2 3 4 5 6 7 8 9 10 07 06 05 04 03

To my dad, Joel Lucke, in memoriam,
and my mom, Nancy Lucke:
your sacrifices have been innumerable;
my gratitude, immeasurable.
—Glenn Lucke

To the authentic worship community of Logos
—Ben Young

Contents

Acknowledgments

AS A FIRST-TIME WRITER, I have an abundance of people to credit and thank:

The Theology Dinner gang (Matthew Brumbelow, Ryan Bower, Katie Ludeman, Brian Rowe, and Sarah Sisti). The conversations in this book have roots in our lively discussions.

Dan Bates, Paul Walker, George Hinman, Sally Connelly, and David Lumpkins read the entire original manuscript very thoroughly and offered excellent, painful criticism. Becca Schwinger, Sandra McCracken, Richmond and Bradley Talbert, Adrienne Flowers, Marian Jordan, Andrea Koeninger, Katie Rooney, Laura Holland, Christina Stone, Rob Douglas, Matthew Pipkin, Colin Hunter, Chuck DeGroat, Dustin Salter, Scott Armstrong, Patrick Connelly, Cat Serna, PJ Lampi, Debbie Elias, Rachel Morris, and Jeff Peck read parts of the book. Faults remain that are mine, but their diligent work made this book vastly different and better. For valuable assistance in background research: Howard Park, Dave Ramazetti, Derek Lewis, Julie Briggs, Caroline Blitzer, Chase Heavener, Laura Towne, and Carolina Cobb.

Richard Pratt, Charles MacKenzie, and the other outstanding faculty at Reformed Theological Seminary–Orlando who were my gifted teachers.

Dr. and Mrs. H. Edwin Young and the entire Second Baptist family. Their fingerprints are all over our lives and thus the book. Toni Richmond, Ben's assistant and my friend, for priceless help. She is the unsung heroine who keeps lives together and ministries humming, all with astonishing grace and excellence.

Caedmon's Call: their lyrics and music have been sustaining grace, their friendship all the more. Derek Webb: for the idea that everything happens on schedule, even stains on a shirt.

Len Goss, Kim Overcash, Mary Beth Shaw, and Paul Mikos at Broadman & Holman Publishers for their diligent work and patience.

Lastly my parents, Joel and Nancy Lucke, who gave everything for their children in the hopes that we might be happy. I hope this small fruit provides a measure of happiness in return.

Soli Deo Gloria,
Glenn Lucke
May 2003

I want to thank the Logos Community at Second Baptist Church for inspiring this work. The core team along with others who make it possible every week: Dr. Gary Peil, my brother Cliff Young, Aaron Senseman, Mark Poe, Lee Ann Ashburn, Sarah Welch, DK Kilgore, Mark Sepulveda, Chris Dahse, Rush Bigger, the entire media team, and Toni Richmond.

Soli Deo Gloria,
Ben Young
May 2003

Preface

THIS BOOK BEGAN as a dream to see the Logos congregation in Houston discover the joy and power of living Christian teachings. At the Logos service, Ben preached through the major teachings of the faith for a solid year, and the enormously positive response was gratifying.

We decided to put the sermons into book form for a wider audience, but somewhere along the way we realized that embedding the teachings in a story seemed like the way Jesus often taught. Also a story seemed like the right sugar to help the medicine of doctrine go down.

Thus, in and around the ensuing story, four Christian doctrines are explained in the dialogue. Study questions for each chapter at the end of the book will help make this a more practical, life-altering experience. Perhaps the best way to experience the book, though, is to read it in a small group or class and talk through the stories, teachings, and study questions together. Hopefully readers will see a vision of God, high and lifted up, and as they think and pray in community, God will show himself high and lifted up in their lives as well.

Chapter 1

A Dangerous Kiss

THE ELEVATOR BECKONED, and the three bankers strode inside and pivoted to face the doors sliding to a close. Dell angled his head slightly to eye his junior colleagues. Brad Masterson felt the gaze come to him, and he turned to meet Dell's. They stared at each other for only three seconds, but long enough for Dell to size up Brad under pressure. The same tight-lipped but confident smile creased both their faces, and their eyes shone.

A few mergers and acquisitions and the occasional IPO were the only blips that evidenced the capital markets were not flatlining. The jitters about terrorism, the uncertainty of the U.S. economy, and the corporate scandals of the past two years—the avalanche of bad news shattered the formerly invincible confidence of the gung ho '90s, leaving in its place the risk-averse millennium.

Tension had increased steadily for weeks, but since the deal team departed the Houston airport two hours ago, the tension had morphed into almost tangible form. Frank Dell, the managing director running this pitch to Aracell Oil & Gas, wanted the deal in a bad way. Dell's eyes fell next on the vice president on the deal, Julian Roth, and Brad saw Julian smile fully. Julian was game.

This is what Julian had taught him; being game was the key. A memory flashed to Brad's mind. During his senior year in high school,

1

he quarterbacked Cadian, taking on arch rival St. James at Rice Stadium. It was *the* game of the season. St. James had won the previous two years, and Brad's senior year St. James again had the more talented team. He was a good-not-great quarterback, but Brad had played the game of his life in that final high school game. In the milliseconds of the staccato memory collage, Brad could see himself calm in the huddle, executing the option, making the throws, leading Cadian to eke out the upset win. As he rose to the next level, his teammates looked at him differently in the huddle. It was the same thing now. Intense pressure, high stakes—you had to be game, both relaxed and high performing.

Brad checked himself in the mirrored glass doors, reassured by the Alden dress shoes and classic Brooks Brothers suit. While some of his counterparts in New York looked down on the old Wall Street standby in favor of trendier sartorial splendor, Brad matched their disdain with his own for their effete Euro-look. His one concession was the Hermés tie.

The elevator whirred toward the upper floors of the Union Tower in New Orleans. Seconds away from arrival, Dell turned to his colleagues and said, as he always did before a pitch.

"Julian, Brad . . . It's *showtime.*"

† † †

A knock sounded at her door. "Ms. Fontenot, here is the document you requested," said Diane, her secretary. Lauren looked up briefly from the various papers already on her desk, which she had arranged while she waited on hold for the secretary on the other end to connect her to the client CFO. She reached out for the new papers from Diane as the client came on line. "Thank you," she mouthed to Diane with a half smile.

Lauren, a third-year associate at Burnam & Krysp, would be "taking comments" in this call, with inevitable rewordings and changes at the CFO's behest. "Yes, Mr. Martin, this is Lauren Fontenot. Hope you're having a good morning. Yes, I have the registration statement in front of me." With the clock running at even her paltry $200 an hour, clients got down to business in a hurry.

To Lauren's surprise, instead of a painstaking session with multiple editing suggestions, Mr. Martin had only a couple of changes he wanted made. Soon he came to the end: "Ms. Fontenot, this is fine. Great work. Fax me the changes, please, as soon as you make them. It's good working with you. Got to go, but I'll be talking to you or Jacobson very soon."

When she depressed the speakerphone button, she glowed with pride. A salary six times what her mom made hardly made up for all the long hours; hearing such appreciation from the client on a measly registration statement definitely did. Lauren reviewed the registration statement on her desk. As a third-year, she possessed a trained eye, and she was beginning to know the elements that comprised an excellent piece of due diligence for an offering deal. She had turned this around quickly for Jacobson, the partner on the deal, which meant the client had received it slightly ahead of time. And now the CFO was pleased. Excellent and quick. Job well-done. This was why she was an attorney. This was life at Burnam & Krysp. A frisson of pleasure shot through her.

Jacobson called. "Lauren, I need those docs for the Diamond Offshore offering in two days. Can you get to them?"

Lauren did a quick mental inventory of which other partners needed what and when. It was going to mean some longer hours, but she enjoyed working with Jacobson. "Yes, I can do it. I'll be pushing it, but it's doable."

She hung up the phone, swiveled in her seat, and stared out her window at another concrete-and-glass structure across the street. Immediately the pleasure of the preceding moment dissipated. For what seemed like the twentieth or thirtieth time in the last two months, a pang of emptiness rattled through her mind, and she felt it in her gut. Why was she here? Why was she doing this? Why did she feel so . . . angry? And why at no one in particular? The temptation to let go and wallow in pity and anger manifested, but as she had done each time in the last two months, she buried the temptation in resolve. *Focus,* she told herself. Buck up! Still, this time she felt emotion swelling more than the other times. What was going on? How could she be sky-high one moment and so low the next? She shook it off.

†††

Seated in the conference room high above downtown New Orleans, Brad didn't allow himself to admire the view outside the window. He smiled to himself at the perfunctory graciousness of the Aracell CEO. Some executives looked up to bankers or at least admired them in some way. Others viewed Brad and his colleagues with suspicion. This one, Jack Schor, was neither an old client nor even a friend of Dell's, and Schor managed to disguise any admiration well. Still, he and his executive team sat back and listened as Dell opened the meeting.

Brad liked Dell quite a bit, and he really liked Roth. Julian was probably the best guy in the firm. Still . . . Brad was fascinated to see how the power aura that framed Dell and Julian in their Houston offices now shriveled before the impatient intelligence of the Aracell execs. Dell was larger than life to the associates in the investment bank, and even to the VPs, but here Schor dwarfed him in personality. Amazing.

According to their pre-scripted presentation, Julian took over and guided them through the next few pages of the pitch book. The meeting was going OK.

†††

Lauren couldn't shake the fear she felt at this most recent bout of emptiness. It was getting worse. She couldn't tell Brad or Jarrod. Her mom had enough problems, and for almost two decades Lauren had known she had to be strong for her.

Why was this happening? She was doing good work, billing a lot of hours, working out. She had a great loft in the old Rice Hotel, good friends, and she enjoyed the attentions of the many guys who asked her out. What was wrong? But she'd been asking herself these questions for around two months and reminding herself of her portfolio of good reasons why everything was fine. Everything wasn't fine, and she felt her ability to resist the gravitational pull diminishing. Darkness crept around the edges of her life perspective. Life was still sunny, but the thickening blackness on the edge of her mind's eye portended worse things.

Lauren sat back in her chair and swiveled around. Her independent streak, the reliable answer to most of life's challenges, wasn't helping. But whom could she talk to about this? She thought of Annette, one of her Chi Omega friends from college who was working for another big firm in Houston. The social scene constantly swirled around Annette, and she had this magical gift for always knowing just what to say. Plus, even though Annette was a trial attorney, she was a total softie with her friends. She would be a good listening ear and maybe would have some clue about what was going on.

Lauren dialed Annette's direct line but felt panic as it rang. When Annette answered, Lauren asked, "Annette, I need to talk to you. If you're busy, we can talk later."

"What's wrong, Lauren?" Annette asked. "We can talk longer later, but I do have a few minutes right now if you want to talk."

Lauren felt embarrassed to admit what was going on, for she was the strongest one of all their sorority friends. But the fear that something inexplicable inside was spiraling down overcame her embarrassment, and she briefed Annette on the bouts of emptiness and irritability.

Annette listened quietly, then asked a few clarifying questions. "Lauren, I know you're not going to want to hear this, but I really think you should go see Dr. Ffeir. Before you say no, let me tell you about him. A lot of my friends have seen him. He's one of the best therapists in Houston."

"You mean a shrink?" asked Lauren incredulously. "I'm not crazy. I just need someone to help me figure out what's going on."

"Lauren, trust me. I know this is hard, but he's really good. My friends talk about him all the time. I feel like I know him."

"But this is so weird. I just need some perspective. I'm not sick or crazy."

"Lauren, it's not like that. Have you talked to Maddy recently? She says everyone in Manhattan has a therapist. Even here, I probably hear a story from a friend every month at lunch or at a bar about what her therapist is telling her to do. It's so normal. It's actually crazy *not* to see one. We all need perspective, as you said. Dr. Ffeir can really help."

"You're sure this is normal? If I do this, you won't tell *any*one?"

"Completely! Of course I won't say a word. Give him a call. I have his number in my Rolodex. Hold on."

Lauren couldn't believe she was contemplating doing this, but she felt a flutter of hope. If she could just have a name for whatever this thing was that afflicted her, then she could definitely trample it. She'd be back to normal soon.

† † †

The Aracell team asked a few questions, and then the next flip of the page signaled Brad's part of the presentation.

"Tom asked me to review the model I've prepared." Brad loved this part, when the graphics and numbers on the page—numbers he knew intimately from long hours spent doing the due diligence—became a story to tell. He quickly reviewed the assumptions as he ran through the summary pages in the pitch book that laid out the financial condition of the company.

"You see how we've factored in these earnings and cash-flow expectations for this year and the year after."

Schor nodded. "These are in line with our own expectations."

Brad continued, "Based on our expectations of your capital spending over the next two years . . ."

If you knew the business and knew the numbers, and Brad did, they became notes that created a familiar song that all around the table recognized and liked. Dell, Julian, and Brad simply played the chords. Brad smiled to himself, remembering a Jerry Jeff Walker show at Gruene Hall, because the meeting became sing-along with the Aracell team. As Brad finished, Schor said, "Son, you might actually earn that Hermés tie someday." Everyone laughed, and the light hazing signaled that he had done well.

† † †

Back in the Richmond Steinberg offices, Brad paused before diving into the pile of work awaiting him. In three minutes he narrated the Aracell war story to the other associates, who congratulated him before promptly returning to their monitors and phones. With dozens of pitch books in their recent past and hundreds more in their certain future, no one had time for more than cursory celebration. Brad, however, privately enjoyed the afterglow of the successful meeting.

Then the phone rang, and the glow diminished for a while. Brad involuntarily clinched as the VP on the other end, Carville, sketched the outlines of another marketing deal. This meant four active deals on his plate, and things were supposed to be slow. The VP reminded Brad that they all needed to scrounge a bit, trying harder than usual to create new business.

Brad didn't like working with Carville. The associates in the bank possessed uncanny antennae for office politics, and with attrition a constant each year, the sly scuttlebutt said this VP's career at the bank was listing to port. No one was more aware than Jameson Carville, and he was not going down without a fight. His stripping down the associates had been going beyond the usual culture of accepted abuse, and his demands for turnaround time on projects exceeded the normal insanity. Since associates and analysts were "variable costs" in a bad economy and since banks were notoriously unsentimental about people, Carville's ship taking on water could pull nearby smaller ships into the drowning vortex. Brad and the other junior people duly ratcheted up their work for him.

The main reason Brad stiffened was because building a model for Carville's proposed deal for Sparling Oil meant less time to focus on an interesting deal he was working on with Julian. Three weeks ago Julian had called Brad into his office to give him the game plan for an acquisition pitch to a successful exploration firm, Spinnaker Exploration. Julian, without explicit mention, took Brad under his wing and began mentoring him. Like any other midlevel associate, Brad tired of the routine of making pitch books, hungering for more responsibility. Julian sketched the game plan for Spinnaker and told Brad he needed him to step up on this one. Message received. In two days, if this new Sparling marketing pitch didn't drain too much time, Brad would deliver his work to Julian on Spinnaker.

After Carville released him from the phone, Brad permitted himself a moment of reflection. Of the few things in his social life, Brad had let most of them slide these previous weeks. He had gone to church with his family at Inwood Drive Baptist, and he'd had lunch with them afterward. But he had cancelled a tennis match with a high school friend, declined two golf outings, an Astros baseball game, and entirely blown off his weight-lifting routine. He'd still managed to run four times a week because that helped him maintain equilibrium. The one thing he had really missed was the coffeehouse with Lauren and Jarrod. It had been more than a month since he'd made it, and this was supposed to be a slow time in the world of investment banking. But he had to get this Spinnaker deal done expertly and soon. A lot rode on this.

Still, Lauren flitted around the edges of his consciousness more than ever. Whatever attraction Brad felt when he first met her their freshman year, he had sublimated all these years. She was off-limits, and they had simply, along with Jarrod, become great friends. Sometimes his radar would pick up a look from Lauren that lasted a fraction of a second longer than normal, or he would catch her looking at him across the coffee shop when he was getting refills for all of them. But most of the time, she clearly was his friend and that was it. They were just too different. Great friends, but it simply couldn't be more. With all the pressure on him now, and the special opportunity that Julian was giving him on this Spinnaker deal, with less sleep than ever, why was he having thoughts of Lauren now? It made no rational sense, but he couldn't deny that the moments when Lauren intruded on his thoughts were good ones.

† † †

Lauren initially couldn't believe her good fortune, that a late cancellation meant she could get in to see Ffeir for his last session of the day at six. Since the session had begun, however, she had had cause to reconsider whether her fortune was good.

"Rational?" asked Dr. Ffeir. "Why do you say *rational?*"

"Because . . . you have to be smart about these things," responded Lauren. Her brow furrowed as her eyes narrowed.

"Sure. OK. I hear you." Dr. Ffeir faced her squarely in the chair, and his head bobbed up and down a little too quickly to be sincere. Lauren thought back to Annette, who had said Ffeir came highly recommended as one of the best counselors in downtown Houston, but Lauren was starting to think he was only a caricature of a human being. "So what you're saying, Lauren, is that you want to be smart about relationships."

Irritability rose in her throat. "Yes," she answered in a clipped manner, her mouth barely operating beyond clenched position. "That is what I already said."

What rival attorneys could never do to her even in intense negotiations, this counselor was achieving in half an hour. Her hand came up to her forehead and remained there. She sighed, exasperated.

"Look, I need help thinking through this. Perspective. As I told you, I've been aware of a strange feeling for months now. I don't think it has to do with my friends Brad or Jarrod. Yes, I sometimes have feelings of attraction for them, more often Brad, but those are rare times. I don't *want* to think about Brad that way; I don't even want to talk about my feelings about Brad. And I'm certainly not going to talk to *him* about those rare, occasional occurrences of attraction, because it's not rational, not smart. Doctor, we're off course talking about Brad. I didn't come hear to talk about friendships or dating. I came for help with this sense of unhappiness that I can't shake. Can we please stick to that?"

Lauren noted, with a twinge of guilty pleasure, that Dr. Ffeir reddened slightly and looked down at his hands, then removed his glasses to wipe them before replacing them on his nose. All this, she knew from postnegotiation debriefs with older associates and partners, was just buying time to compose himself to the point where he could look her in the eye again. She wasn't happy about knocking him off his patronizing high horse, but she was happy to regain control of this session and get things focused on what would help her. Spending $250 an hour for him to repeat statements back to her was a joke. She could buy a parrot for one-tenth that amount.

Dr. Ffeir was finally ready to venture another question. "Would you say, Lauren, that you are frustrated?"

This time the irritation flared all the way to her head. Crossly, she answered, "Yes! Yes, that's exactly what I am, frustrated! I'm frustrated that I'm spending time *here* when you're not focusing on what I told you was the issue. I'm frustrated that you're repeating back what I say. Can you do *anything* to help figure this out?"

This time Ffeir volleyed back. "I understand your frustration, Lauren." He nodded sympathetically. "I really do. And I'm trying to help. But sometimes what people think is *the* issue turns out to mask deeper, underlying issues that really are the source of anxiety. Your feelings of unhappiness may be related to work, maybe not. Maybe they are related to your life outside of work, maybe not. And *maybe* you are at a point in life in which you have some unfulfilled longings in the area of intimacy, so exploring questions about attractions, your friend Brad, and your relationship with him is all part of unearthing what *might* be causing your unhappiness."

Mollified, Lauren replied, "OK. Yes, I can believe that relationship matters might cause someone unhappiness. But I'm happy in my relationships with Brad and Jarrod and my other friends. I date quite a bit, and I've enjoyed the guys I've dated. I understand your taking this tack, but I assure you, this is not it. My unhappiness is not related to my friends or unfulfilled longings for Brad or any other guy. There's just something not right in my life. Something's off, and I don't know what it is."

The session went on another twenty minutes, Ffeir listening to Lauren speculate what might be causing her recent sense of being unsettled. Lauren should have known better, for she billed in six-minute increments, and if a client was so stupid as to take control, she always let him. Whoever said talk is cheap didn't bill by the hour. But she felt better having spoken her mind about the problem. Another session was scheduled.

† † †

Brad looked at the clock, saw that it was 7:30, and realized he was hungry. He clicked on the Excel worksheet and corrected a formula. Hungry, *and* he wanted to see Lauren. The afterglow from today's performance in New Orleans returned, and he was feeling his oats. At the same time he was dog tired. And he *missed* Lauren.

He didn't even think about it. He punched the speakerphone and dialed her mobile.

"Lauren?"

"Brad!" She sounded strangely effusive.

"What's going on?"

"Not much, just shopping."

And she claims that corporate attorneys work just as hard as investment bankers, he thought.

"I was thinking that we haven't gotten together in a while, and I've got some time free later. Any interest in meeting up at Charley's 517 for a late dessert?"

"Hmm . . . that sounds inviting. How late were you thinking?"

"9:30?"

"That works well. I'm going to head back to the Rice and take care of some things there, but that will be fine. Thanks, Brad. I'll see you there."

† † †

Brad loved the place for its sumptuous ambience. Remembering the old Bum Phillips line about running back Earl Campbell, Brad thought Charley's 517 may not be in a class by itself, but it doesn't take long to call the roll. As far as he was concerned, it was the best restaurant downtown. Lauren tucked into her tiramisu, but Brad leisurely picked at the tres leches cake. The replays of his performance at the Aracell meeting and the sight of lovely Lauren jacked him up again. Though physically depleted, his spirits soared. And he felt *attracted.* No, there was definitely no rush tonight. He wanted to enjoy all this, and he wanted to enjoy her.

He nodded and smiled broadly when she told about her client's appreciation. "We've both had good days," he said.

Lauren wanted to say, *No, you have no idea how bad it's been,* but Dr. Ffeir's question now reappeared, unbidden. What about Brad? She knew they both had danced around flare-ups in chemistry since midway through college, and despite his Neanderthal religious beliefs, she welcomed the interest. He had always played it safe, though, which was probably best for the friendship but tweaked her ego since he seemed unavailable for unknown reasons. But tonight he looked at her differently, with almost a driven quality. Brad's restraint, imbued in all Mastersons, suffered spider-web cracks before her eyes.

"Yes, we are having good days," she smiled back, slowly closing and opening her eyes and moving her head slightly.

For whatever silly reason that smile and that movement got him. The attraction whipped at him, leaving a feeling in his gut and neck like the sensation of wispy tentacles lacerating him with an inebriating bite. As the sharp stimulation subsided, he found it followed by a formidable pull toward her. Without a drop of alcohol, he felt buzzed.

She felt the same pull. Any other time in their long friendship she would have said, "Brad, what are we doing?" A faraway voice in her mind asked as much, but she paid it no attention. He was Brad Masterson— handsome, wealthy, achieving, smart, fun, and from a great family. And finally he was interested in more than being friends. Why not? She swatted away a final entreaty from the voice of reason. Why not?

† † †

Brad reached for Lauren's hand as they exited and began the short walk to her loft at the Rice Hotel. They didn't speak but glanced at each other from time to time as they strolled. When they arrived upstairs and reached her door, the expected awkwardness never came. They both knew.

Brad leaned down and kissed her gently, quickly on the lips. He straightened up, both of them grinning. Then Brad reached out with both arms and pulled Lauren in for a long kiss.

After she disengaged, she tiptoed up to his ear and whispered, "Thank you. Good-night." He stood there watching her let herself in the door, shaking his head slightly in amazement. Lauren winked, before she finally turned, walked in, and began to close the door behind her.

"I'll call you tomorrow," he said, glowing.

† † †

Brad awoke with a hangover, though he never drank. In this case it was more a case of chemistry run amok. The clarity and pleasure of incipient romance with Lauren the night before gave way to sorrow and regret. *What was I thinking!* he inwardly yelled at himself. They were *friends.* They could never date seriously. She despised the most important thing in his life—his faith. He'd always kept everything straight with her because of it, and now that was all ruined.

God, why did this happen? Shoot! Now he was going to have to tell Lauren. He cringed inwardly, foreseeing her mushrooming anger. This was going to stink. How did this ever come to happen?

And then it hit him. He was also going to have to tell Jarrod.

† † †

"You must be kidding. You are calling me the day *after* you kiss me to tell me that this is not a good idea? You tell me this *now?*" Fury distorted her face as she hurled Brad's words back at him. "We go all these years as friends, you make a play for something more, and *now* you take it back? That's wrong. You can't do that. Brad Masterson, I *cannot* believe you are doing this."

"Lauren, I don't know what else to say. I guess . . . I'll say it again. I am sorry. I really am. I don't know what got into me. You're right; we have kept everything straight for years. I didn't mean to hurt you."

"What do you mean you don't know what got into you?" her tone seared, as intended. "Like you're clueless today about why you liked me last night?"

"No, no, nothing like that. Lauren, I think you're great. It's not that."

"Please tell me you have a reason, Brad. Please tell me you're not calling me the next morning after we kiss to tell me that we have to just be friends for *no reason.* I *need* a reason, Brad."

"Lauren, you know this. We've talked about this . . . or I guess around this . . . since we met in Austin."

"What?"

Brad didn't reply.

"What, the religious stuff? You've got to be kidding. You're going to trample all this because of Christianity?"

"Yes."

"Brad, what on earth does religion have to do with this and us?"

"Lauren, come on, I know you know this. My faith is the most important thing in life to me. The Bible says we are not to be unequally yoked with unbelievers. Plus, I've been a leader in the church. I know what's expected. Leaders are supposed to set the bar a little higher. I can't date someone who is not a Christian."

"What?! You have *got* to be kidding me. This is a joke! You're judging *me?* You're saying I'm not good enough because I'm not some kind of wacko fundamentalist? After creating this whole thing last night and kissing me, you're telling me that I'm not good enough? I cannot believe you're doing this. This . . ."

Lauren paused, exasperated.

"Brad, I've got to go. I can't deal with this now. I've got to get back to work. Bye." She hung up the phone without waiting for a response. There was no placating her.

Brad looked down at his watch. And this was the easy one, he thought.

He agreed with her too. It wasn't because she wasn't good enough. He felt like a complete heel. But he knew that regardless of what he did last night, today he was doing the right thing.

† † †

"You did what?" Jarrod could not believe Brad's words. "Tell me you're kidding. You did not kiss Lauren."

"Jarrod, I'm sorry. I know it was wrong."

"You were the one who told me I couldn't date her years ago!"

"Jarrod, I know. That was the right advice all along. I just slipped up."

"I just can't believe you'd ruin a friendship like that. And betray me. This looks so bad, Brad. It *is* so bad. We've talked about this from time to time. Why change now? You were adamant in the past."

1 5

"I don't know. I screwed up. I can't answer this. I just know that I did the wrong thing. I've asked for her forgiveness. She'd rather see me dead than forgiven. And I have to ask for your forgiveness. I'm really sorry. I know this was totally self-serving. I realize that. I just don't know how to make it better."

"Brad, man, your soul is getting dark. This is bad stuff, man. Your heart is getting corrupted. I can't believe you did this."

"Believe me, I can't either." Brad exhaled ponderously for the umpteenth time that day. "I don't know how to get out of this jam. It's going to take a miracle to get out of it."

Chapter 2

Coffee Matters

MIDTOWN HOUSTON conferred an air of charm on the Common Grounds coffee shop. The area, just west of downtown, had a history that stretched back decades, and since the long-neglected area had been rediscovered, it evoked a sense of mystique to the recent college grads who were moving in. New shops in old buildings and refurbished homes maintained the quaint feel even as developers rushed to erect new lofts to meet the housing demand of thousands of young employees working in the downtown skyscrapers that loomed overhead.

Common Grounds capitalized on the trendy mystique of the old-new blend. The coffeehouse had been a restaurant, which, in its heyday of the 1940s, had made a name servicing lunch-hour businessmen and white-gloved ladies shopping at the downtown department stores. As the neighborhood fell into decline, the restaurant was sold to a succession of owners and mirrored the growing dilapidation of the surroundings. Recent revitalization efforts and the influx of hip twenty-somethings with hefty disposable incomes fairly necessitated a coffeehouse, so a savvy entrepreneur turned the venerable restaurant into Common Grounds.

Brad, Lauren, and Jarrod sat uneasily around a table in Common Grounds, the site of their Sunday evening get-togethers. They aimed at twice a month, but Brad's schedule—if it could legitimately be called a schedule—meant he missed more than a few rendezvouses. Sunday nights at Common Grounds had evolved into Lauren and Jarrod meeting, with Brad showing up if he could take an hour away from work.

The rancor felt by all three from the episode with Brad and Lauren lingered, though they had officially talked through it, and Brad had apologized to both. Jarrod's accusation about Brad's increasingly calloused heart stung Brad, because he knew it was at least partially true. He'd been doing a lot of thinking, and an experience at church that morning had related to the whole mess in a surprising way. Brad was excited to talk about this new development, but he suspected his friends were not ready for his surprise on the heels of the recent unpleasantness.

Lauren's detachment belied the pronouncement that she considered this all water under the bridge. *She is too smart,* Brad thought, *to play it cold.* Coldness would be too obvious. But her slight aloofness, her less frequent and briefer eye contact, told Brad that she was still angry. They both surmised that Jarrod's unease came from the uncomfortable present situation. While he didn't sweep stuff under the rug with either of them, he was able to forgive and had already let things go.

After several false starts at aimless chitchat, Lauren finally moved to get the conversation going. "Brad, what is it?" Lauren asked. "Something's got you keyed up."

Brad smiled. "Think about all the times we've discussed faith matters since we first met. It's a big part of my life and Jarrod's life. And Jarrod was right the other day. I have become hardened." Looking at Jarrod, he said, "I don't really want to agree with what you said about my becoming 'darker,' but the more I've thought about it, the less I am able to argue with you. Something *is* amiss. In a nutshell, God really hasn't been on my mind that much lately. This is not because of your old critique that my church is dead. It has a lot more to do with me and work. I've not been into my faith as much recently. But . . . I feel like that's changed today."

"So what's the deal?" Jarrod inquired. "What's got you going?"

"This morning at church we had a guest preacher. He was really special. His name is Dr. MacGregor, and he gave an intriguing message."

"Intriguing?" asked Lauren.

"He talked about Ecclesiastes, this Old Testament book. It was deep. I felt like he was talking directly to me, like he had been reading my mail. All this stuff about meaninglessness in life. The guy who wrote Ecclesiastes did it all—money, power, sex—and it was all meaningless. What hit me was how caught up *I've* been in work, how I've been chasing all these other things, but to what purpose? The questions alone that this guy asked in his sermon nailed me. He had a way of asking questions that personalized for me every point that he made and every story that he told."

"Nailed?" queried Lauren archly.

"Well, 'nailed' as if God was saying, 'Wake up! Remember me? You're not living for me anymore.' It shook me up. I've been on autopilot in my faith for a while, and I didn't even realize it. This guy hit me right between the eyes."

"Was he preaching at you? It sounds like he came on awfully strong to me," said Lauren, always ready to be suspicious of religious leaders, especially from Brad's world of Southern Baptists.

"No, no, no. He was actually laid back most of the time, just telling the story of Solomon as he went through Ecclesiastes. I felt meaningless, but I also felt hope. A load was lifted. I got excited, like, 'Oh yeah. This is what it's like to be tracking with the Lord.' It was the first time I've been excited in church in a while."

A satisfied smile came over Jarrod's face, and Brad rolled his eyes in response.

"Oh, get off it. It had to do with *me* not being focused on God, not my church. Anyway, I went up to him after the service and told him how much I appreciated what he said. He was great, really nice. I told him that we get together and sometimes have discussions about God and how we have tackled some tough questions over the years. He seemed really interested and kept asking questions about you and what we talk about, so eventually I thought he might actually want to meet you. So I basically invited him to join us. I hope it's alright with you if we chat with him, because he said he would come."

"*Here?* To the coffee shop?" Lauren responded, incredulous.

"Yeah. He should be here any minute. Wouldn't it be great to ask him some of the questions we've wrestled with in the past?"

Lauren, wary, looked at Jarrod to gauge his reaction. Jarrod shrugged. "You know me. Always up for meeting new people, and I love a stimulating conversation."

He and Brad now looked back at Lauren. "Well, what do you say?" asked Brad.

"Maybe," replied Lauren, "but what expertise does he have?" Having secured her own credentials with hard work and after working in the legal world of evidence and experts, Lauren wasn't about to accept some stranger without contest. Especially any religious person who would speak at Brad's kind of unenlightened church.

"I'm sure his having a 'doctor' before his name means a Ph.D. in theology or Old Testament or New Testament or something. When introducing him, the pastor said that he teaches at the seminary, and he kept referring to him as 'Professor MacGregor.'"

That more than satisfied Jarrod, and while the new information seemingly addressed Lauren's challenge, she was hardly mollified. Not that there was much that she could do, and she knew it. While she relished intellectual *contre temps* as much as any educated person, she was always skittish about religion in general and certainly wary of the particular brand of religion espoused by Brad and Jarrod. But if Brad's stranger was already en route to meet them, any objection she had at this late notice would look rude and unsociable. *Might as well get on the welcome wagon,* she thought.

The sense of unease still hovered, though only faintly now, as though Brad's contrition about "the episode" last week and his current excitement for his new friend had pushed it back. But now a new awkwardness had been introduced. They weren't really through dealing with the rupture of the previous week, and they had not yet had time to rebuild trust. Lauren felt this was all a bit brusque, and she guessed Jarrod felt a bit of the same, but he also seemed interested in meeting this mystery figure.

Soon thereafter, Brad's guest arrived. MacGregor walked into Common Grounds, ducking a bit as he passed through the door frame, and searched around for Brad. He looked quite a bit older than most of the coffeehouse addicts (Brad guessed about sixty-five), and grey hair had already made a steady march from his temples toward the crown of his head, leaving a remnant of black hair under siege. Overall, Lauren thought he looked surprisingly lean and fit for his age, though his midsection showed signs of thickening. MacGregor wore a blue blazer, dark grey slacks, and white dress shirt, but no tie.

"Perhaps," wondered Jarrod wryly, "not wearing a tie is his attempt at being casual in our trendy coffee shop." Before Brad or Lauren could comment, Brad caught the professor's eye, and they all stood to greet him as he walked over to their table. They exchanged greetings, and Brad repeated his association from that morning's church service, more for the professor's benefit. After shaking their hands and getting their names, the professor said, "I am Charles MacGregor, and I'm delighted to meet you. I look forward to getting to know each of you better." He didn't just smile; he beamed, and the wrinkles on his face showed that he smiled often. His blue-grey eyes flooded with warmth, and they, three young professionals, each had the sensation that before them was a kind man. They couldn't help but smile in return.

"I'm going to order something to drink, and I'll be right back, if you'll excuse me." After he had walked away, Jarrod shrugged and said, "Seems nice." Lauren nodded, and Brad said, "I know. He *is* really nice. And sharp. I can't wait to get him talking about all our past debates."

"Brad, I thought this was about you reconnecting with God after becoming such a jerk of late. Are you sure debates about beliefs are what we need?" asked Jarrod.

Brad thought for a second, but before he could answer, MacGregor returned with a scone and tea and sat down. "Thank you for having me. I'm honored to be invited to join you tonight. Brad mentioned that you have been getting together and having discussions for years. Why don't you fill me in on your story—when you met and all that?"

Lauren began the narrative. "I guess you could say we are old college friends. We were in the same dorm our freshman year at the University of Texas." She smiled, Jarrod smiled, and so did Brad. Just beginning the reminiscing banished the remnant uneased and rekindled the old warmth.

"Brad is the picture of a high-octane achiever from a whole family of achievers. He beat out most of our friends and landed a plumb job as an analyst with Richmond Steinberg, a big investment bank with a Houston office." Brad's appearance for this casual evening at Common Grounds confirmed Lauren's description. He wore natty linen summer khaki slacks, woven calfskin Cole Haan loafers, and a pale yellow golf shirt bearing the insignia of Royal St. Andrews in Scotland. Brad had gained a little weight since college, and though he remained fairly thin, he was slightly too muscular to be called lanky. Seated in his chair, offset from the table so he could cross his legs, Brad exuded that quintessential Texan air that was equal parts patrician and good old boy camaraderie.

"The fact that his dad knows four of the managing directors had nothing to do with it," Jarrod added.

"Of course not," continued Lauren. "He did all kinds of things that those curious creatures called 'analysts' do, but increasingly he worked more with the Energy Group, which specialized in mergers and acquisitions. Am I reproducing your party spiel from a few years ago, Bradley?"

Brad smiled graciously but rolled his eyes at the professor as the infomercial with mocking tone continued.

"The taste of doing deals and the lure of the huge year-end bonuses brought young Brad back to the firm after he got his MBA at UT. You should have heard him before he went to business school; he was one *bitter* entry-level analyst. You'd think they had repealed the Emancipation Proclamation and the Thirteenth Amendment to hear him tell stories about work. Somewhere I suppose there is a gun to his head; I just can't see it.

"Now that he's back at the firm as a second-year associate with his MBA, he doesn't feel any less busy than when he was an entry-level analyst. And surprise, he's *still* bitter. He craves more responsibility in working on deals, so he sticks it out. It's all about doing deals. Deal-making is in his blood. *That* sums him up nicely."

"Very nicely," chimed in Jarrod.

"Hey, all I can say is that if you were up until three in the morning pleading with the copy center to finish your pitch books, you'd be bitter too."

"Brad, this isn't a court of law. You don't have the right to defend yourself here. In front of your new friend, Professor MacGregor, we are the prosecutors, judge, and jury. Besides, it's your own fault that you don't have a life. Take your medicine like a good boy." Lauren clearly enjoyed sticking it to Brad. MacGregor took in all the sparring with a bemused smile.

"Now I'll do Lauren," said Jarrod. "She got into the honors program at UT, and from our first semester in the dorm, Brad and I were pretty impressed with her intelligence. There's actually a lot of similarity between Lauren and Brad in terms of having this strong drive to suc-ceed. The difference is that Brad's drive is just his family's norm—it's what they all just *do*—but Lauren's drive comes from her family having nothing. Her life pretty much stunk, you know, wrecked home and all. She and her sister had to work to help their mom make it."

MacGregor looked at Lauren, who nodded. "Yep, it was definitely tough. As a teenager I scraped and worked to help pay bills, *and* on the way I earned an academic scholarship to UT." As close as she was to Brad and Jarrod, Lauren had never told them the whole story about her family, only that her parents split up. MacGregor nodded understandingly, and Jarrod resumed his take on Lauren.

According to Jarrod, the scraping hadn't erased the sweetness that seemed the native inheritance of Southerners, but Lauren's innate spunk could become a sharp edge when needed. While Jarrod possessed a greater love for things philosophical, Lauren had the most formidable intellect in the group. Her incisive questions and commentary provided much of the spark of their freshman-year bull sessions about politics, religion, movies, and philosophy. Four years of the honors program, followed by three years at law school, had only refined her critical faculties. Lauren was becoming an accomplished associate in corporate law, and while the partner track at her big downtown firm was a challenge for all of her colleagues, she had already begun to distinguish herself.

As Jarrod wound down, Lauren reached out and touched him on the arm and mouthed, "Thank you," with a flirty smile. Jarrod's tale was pleasing to hear.

"I bet your intelligence, education, and legal pursuits make for a fun and tenacious sparring partner at Common Grounds," said MacGregor to Lauren. Brad and Jarrod hastened to agree.

"Don't let Jarrod fool you, Professor. He is equal to the task. He is no slouch when it comes to our discussions and debates." But then Brad wondered aloud, "Should I present Jarrod?"

"Whatever," said Jarrod. "It's all good."

"There we have the first thing I can tell you. Jarrod, or J-Rod as his wakeboarding friends call him, is Mr. Laid Back." The frayed jeans and flip flops betrayed his wakeboarding past, but the button down tropical shirt was more in keeping with his recent position as a programmer for Compaq. Jarrod shrugged his shoulders.

"However, his family is like mine, into achievement—"

Jarrod interrupted, "But Brad, come on. We've talked about this so many times. My family is *not* like your family."

Jarrod looked at MacGregor. "My parents are the insatiable social-climber sort. You would not believe the degree of calculation and pretense. It drives me crazy."

"What do you mean?" asked MacGregor.

"They look around at what everyone else is doing. They look around at what cool rich people are doing, and then they go after it. I mean, it really is ridiculous. Who they invite over for dinner . . . they sit around discussing whether they can get so-and-so to come over, and what it will mean for them to get invited to so-and-so's New Year's Eve party. That kind of stuff."

MacGregor's brows rose a bit in surprise at such a description.

"Oh, it gets worse. We moved all the time. As their careers kept hitting new levels, we had to move to new houses and neighborhoods."

"That is actually pretty funny," said Lauren to the professor. "One night last year when we all got together, we were talking about this, and I had a map of Houston with me because I was still trying to figure out how to drive around this enormous city. Jarrod showed us on the map where his various houses were as he grew up. First they lived way out west in the suburbs near Katy, then they moved to just outside the Beltway. Then they moved into the tony Memorial Villages, but I can't remember which one."

"Piney Point, but it was an older ranch-style house that wasn't even as big as guest houses in Memorial these days."

"Then they made the big jump to prime real estate in West University. So we sat there looking at the map and laughing as Jarrod traced this line from Katy all the way to West U. They just kept moving up the zip code status hierarchy."

"It's true. My family is different from Brad's. When we were at UT, I went home with Brad during the first summer break, and meeting his family was a revelation. They are very, very cool."

Lauren added, "Professor, it's like this: the Mastersons exude all the positive aspects of an established, successful family. Their home, the way they carry themselves, there's just this air of confidence . . . and success . . . and what I call 'settledness.' They've been here a long time, and they're going to be here a long time.

"But here's the thing—it's not obnoxious or off-putting at all. It seems *so* natural. They just do everything with an ease and grace that is entirely winsome. Jarrod's right, they really are amazing. For all the work ethic and civic service, they are genuinely humble. They're really special. I love being around them." As Jarrod and Lauren gave their paeans to his family, Brad looked at his coffee slightly pleased but mostly uncomfortable with such direct comments to them.

"And this is such a jarring contrast to your folks?" inquired MacGregor of Jarrod.

"Oh *yeah*. My folks *live* for the display of success, and they're constantly discussing which restaurant, which store, which vacation is elite. They literally worry *constantly* about this stuff."

"They actually use the word *elite?*" asked MacGregor skeptically.

"No, that's my spin on it," agreed Jarrod. "I suppose they use the same terms we all use, like a 'cool vacation' or 'this restaurant is supposed to be really hot.' But I think my interpretation is exactly spot-on. What is cool or hot to them, in their twisted worlds, means what is elite. They're always angling to get in the IN crowd."

"I suspect they thought you'd be grateful for the comforts and status that their calculations produced," said MacGregor.

"Of course. Instead, they just made me nauseous. I became a total rebel against everything they stood for."

"That's not exactly unusual for a teenager," replied MacGregor with a wink.

"No doubt. And maybe all it was at the time was garden-variety teen rebellion."

Lauren said, "He certainly wasn't the stereotype of a rebel though. They pushed him to play soccer with the children of other professionals, so Jarrod 'rebelled' by playing football and basketball. His parents played golf, so Jarrod took up wakeboarding, which probably defines him as much as anything. They hassled him about making great grades in order to get into a 'name university,' so he blew off his homework. Only his sterling SAT got him into UT."

Brad jumped back in. "At first Jarrod tried *not* to try when it came to school. You know how college is. Skipping classes and hanging out is pretty much the norm, but J-Rod raised it to an art form. He outshined all the others. He was the star slacker and couldn't be bothered with going to class."

Jarrod smiled at the report. "It's true. My parents didn't just give me 'the speech' about making great grades so I could make a lot of money; they gave me *multiple* renditions of it. It was so depressing. College sounded like the salt mines, and Mom and Dad were trying to *inspire* me. There was no way I was going to let the university suck the life out of me the way the system had sucked the life out of them."

"So, did you flunk out?" asked the professor.

"No, ultimately I couldn't cope with the sheer boredom. Basically, my intellectual curiosity itched and itched, and I finally had to scratch it. One day I woke up around noon and turned on the TV like always. I cycled through the entire cable lineup about five times in search of anything interesting. Literally I stopped on the Springer show for a minute and saw the audience chanting 'Jerry, Jerry!' and I marveled at what a waste their lives were to be watching this show in the studio audience. And about two seconds later I realized that the only reason I knew *they* were watching was because *I* was watching the show. The words *transitive property* flashed in my head, and I connected the dots. *My* life was a waste. I was so bored, I actually decided it would be more interesting to go to class than just sit around the dorm room watching anything on TV. And it was."

"Go figure," jabbed Brad.

"Yeah, you have so much room to talk, frat boy."

Lauren stepped in to smooth things over. "Simmer down, boys. Besides incessantly debating Brad and me, mostly Brad, Jarrod pulled a rare double major in computer science and philosophy. Bet you don't know too many people who like philosophy and computer science," she said to MacGregor.

"You'd be surprised," MacGregor replied. "It actually makes a lot of sense."

"Well, he took my advice and went against his own heart in choosing a job with Compaq here in Houston," said Brad.

"Against your heart?" asked the professor in surprised tone. "Why would you go against your own heart with your career?"

"Brad, my parents, and others made a case for getting work experience, making some money, and seeing if programming would actually engage my creative side. My heart said go to grad school in philosophy. But I realized I could always go back to school, I'd have money to pay for it, and I wouldn't be under my parents' thumb. The interesting thing was that I really enjoyed working at Compaq and the challenge of solving problems with the code.

"Yet, ultimately the itch returned, and while I was definitely intellectually challenged by my work at Compaq, my soul was restless. I kept feeling pulled to work on resolving challenges in life, not program code."

"What is your question?" asked MacGregor. Brad and Lauren looked at each other quizzically, for they could tell by the way the professor said *question* that he used it with an unusual meaning.

"As you know, philosophy is the love of wisdom or truth, and what kept itching was this vague project of trying to understand what truth is. We talk about truth all the time, but what is it? How is it that people with totally different positions on an issue can both say that their position is the truth? I figured that the project would become clearer in grad school as I studied with professors, and I hoped I would get some answers. I guess it was a sense of unfinished business that got harder to dismiss."

"Well, that and the fact that Hewlett-Packard bought Compaq and created all kinds of turmoil for the employees," said Brad. "I thought Jarrod did the smart thing. He banked a good deal of cash during his five years to tide him over during grad school, jumped ship before Compaq was officially absorbed into H-P, and then he applied and got accepted to Rice University's graduate program in philosophy."

"So you're at Rice," MacGregor responded enthusiastically. "That's really fine, Jarrod. They have an excellent department."

"Thanks. So far it's a lot of fun but a lot of work. I've never read so much in my life. And it's *all* hard reading, not just some of it."

"The thing is," said Lauren, "is that Jarrod is this really smart guy who reads Kant and Hume, and he gets into the logic and rationality, but it stays locked up in his academic world. He's not that way at all in life. And he's certainly not that way when it comes to religion. We joke about how there's not a shred of rationality in his wild church. He's got this compartment called 'academics and philosophy,' and when he's in that compartment, he's all rationality. Step outside that compartment, and he's laid back, breezy, and emotional. If you heard him talk about what he's reading for class, you'd swear he's Mr. Spock from *Star Trek,* but in life he's about the furthest thing from Spock you can imagine."

MacGregor surveyed Jarrod anew with an intrigued look on his face. "That's not all bad, Jarrod. I'm interested in hearing more about your philosophy studies *and* this wild church. But first, how did you meet and become friends at UT?"

"We lived in the honors dorm," answered Lauren. "I don't even know how we met . . . probably that barbeque that the RAs hosted outside the dorm the first day we moved in. From our first semester we just clicked. We were a slightly unusual set because Brad pledged a fraternity that first semester, and I eventually pledged a sorority the following year. As you probably know, Greeks do so much together that they tend to form their closest relationships with brothers or sisters in their own houses. Somehow Jarrod, even though he never pledged a fraternity, was the glue that bonded us together."

"What fraternity and sorority did you each pledge?" inquired MacGregor.

"Brad pledging Phi Delta Beta was a natural. Jarrod used to tease him about being a Lake Woebegon child and called him 'Above Average Brad.'" The three friends smiled at the memory, and Jarrod winked at MacGregor.

"Well, he was. Professor, look at this specimen before you. He is an above average six feet three inches, and before the ravages of investment banking ruined him, he had above average looks; he was an above average athlete with above average intelligence and above average social class." Brad shook his head helplessly as Jarrod painted his Woebegon picture.

"Yeah, so as you can tell, busting on each other is our primary sport. Only the strong survive," Lauren added gaily. "The truth is, Brad loved being with Jarrod, in spite of all the smack that Jarrod dished out. They even managed to spend time together when Brad strained to make it through that first semester of weed-out classes and pledging."

"I've heard stories for years about pledging at UT," agreed MacGregor. "Only Special Forces training is worse."

"Don't get me wrong," replied Jarrod. "The Phi Delts were great guys, but during the fall semester most other priorities receded in favor of 'educating' their pledges. Those first few months Brad received a good dose of education." Again the three grinned at the memory.

"I stopped having flashbacks only when I graduated and started working," said Brad.

"Yeah, but only because your slave drivers don't allow you enough time for REM sleep. If you ever go on vacation, those hideous nightmares are going to get uncorked all over again." Jarrod was on a roll.

"What puzzles me," mused Lauren, "is how to distinguish Brad as pledge from Brad as associate i-banker? I think he's got it far worse now. Minus the cattle prods."

"Minus the cattle prods," agreed Brad. "Well, and the bank pays slightly more than the fraternity." That's how Brad trumped Jarrod and Lauren in many an exchange. His salary loomed as this almost supernatural yet material entity with its own fiendish life force. It existed separately from Brad, goaded him in his indentured servitude, and yet validated his nonlife to all his peers. For the moment it seemed to justify even the absence of REM sleep.

Lauren spoke up again. "I researched the university's social scene right after I won the scholarship my senior spring in high school. The initial report depressed me: from all I could tell, while only about 10 percent of the students in Austin were Greeks, the fraternities and sororities dominated the social life. Greeks were it.

"Worse, I found out that a person's background was a major factor. The more I found out about the sorority system, I realized that coming from a lower-class background in Louisiana all but guaranteed that I would never be invited to join a sorority. I could rush, but I'd be cut right away."

"But you can never count Lauren out. She's gritty. That determination she brings to everything in life created this amazing resolve to give it her best shot," said Jarrod.

"Lauren was not exactly without assets," Brad pointed out. He and Jarrod painted a vivid picture of Lauren's quest to join a sorority. At five feet seven inches with blue eyes and beautiful dark brown hair, Lauren was attractive. Even more, her vivacity and warmth drew people in. She was self-aware enough to know that with some luck, her gift with people and persistence might just open doors. Learning that she'd never get far without recommendations, and understanding that she simply didn't know sorority alumnae in her poor part of Baton Rouge, she decided on an alternative route. Lauren simply dedicated her freshman year to grades, extracurriculars, and great relationships with students from a myriad of organizations. Her plan worked. Lauren embraced college life with all her characteristic élan, and during her sophomore year, with her new and loyal friends at the Chi Omega house going to bat for her, she pledged.

The professor listened to all this with great interest. "Lauren, that is quite a story. I do know something of the UT fraternity and sorority scene from having so many friends tell stories over the years. Frankly, I am amazed that you were able to pull it off."

"It is kind of amazing. After I was on the other side of rush as a new sister, I became *really* amazed. The whole rush process—wow." She paused. "Well, there's no reason to get all negative in this conversation. Let's talk more about Jarrod. I love describing Jarrod to my girlfriends." According to Lauren, Jarrod brought his own cool to the group—that insouciance typical of surfers and wakeboarders. He looked the part, as much as Brad looked his. Blonde, truly handsome, and giving off that vibe of unperturbed acceptance of any situation, Jarrod was charismatic. *Everyone* in the honors dorm—jocks, geeks, Goths—loved him because Jarrod effortlessly loved them. He played intramural sports with the jocks, worked in the computer lab with the geeks, and hung out with the Goths. He was just easy to be around.

"But as you'll see, that ease doesn't make his mind shut off," said Brad.

"Still, it's different," said Lauren. "Jarrod is just not wired to be critical and argumentative like Brad and I are, though he *can* become that way if he's really interested in a subject. Or if he's pushed. Or if he's in that academic philosophy compartment. Also, Jarrod is refreshingly unafraid to shoot from the hip with us if he sees or hears something that he thinks is out of line."

"Like what?" inquired MacGregor.

"Well, for example, he and Brad got along great in college, but from the beginning Jarrod needled Brad about his elitism."

"Whoa, whoa, whoa!" said Jarrod. "You make it sound like I thought Brad was a jerk."

"It's not that, Jarrod. I totally agree with Lauren. It's just something about you. You are sort of constitutionally wired to side with the weak against the powerful."

"Right," said Lauren. "That's it. And since Brad regularly gives evidence that he values the strong and successful, Jarrod jabs Brad about arrogating himself and his friends above ordinary people."

Jarrod looked at the professor and nodded. "That's true. I believe it's good to have a healthy awareness of and distance from anything that separates you from normal people, and Brad and his above average friends sometimes seem to *try* to be separate from normal people."

"Of course," Lauren opined, "I thought Jarrod was separated from normal people, even more than Brad as a Phi Delt, when it came to religion. Religion cropped up in our freshman year discussions early and often, and we still occasionally circle around to religious topics when we meet here."

"The first time a religious topic came up, I thought Brad was definitely one of those weird Christians like I'd known in Baton Rouge, but that was before Jarrod gave his two cents." It was now Jarrod's turn to roll his eyes and shake his head.

Brad said, "Here we go."

Lauren grinned and returned her gaze to MacGregor. "Without question Jarrod had and has the strangest religious views of anyone I have personally met. Remember what I said about the rationality compartment zone? Jarrod's church is hermetically sealed off from Jarrod's rationality compartment. They are worlds apart."

Brad deadpanned that he thought himself to be the normal one in the group. He told MacGregor how he grew up in a family of Southern

Baptists, and some in his family tree had been pastors. Several generations in Houston led to the family's becoming established, wealthy, and inextricably linked to one of the old Southern Baptist churches in town. In Brad's outlook he was part of an unchanging group of believers who traced their faith back to the Bible. And it was so American too!

"Here's the bottom line," said Lauren. "Brad's family combines all these things that a lot of people can't. They are sober minded, but they're also fun loving. They're hardworking but generous. And they're big into being responsible for themselves, but they're also eager to serve others. Like I said before, I love his family."

"That's all well and good," Jarrod interjected, "but Brad knows— he's been *reared* to know—that his family and his church 'do it right.' If there's one area where they are slightly off-putting, it's this. For the Mastersons, people are supposed to be a certain way, and they *are* that way."

Brad winced. "Um, that's a bit overdrawn. Come on. Give me a break. It's not that bad."

"I don't know about that either," said Lauren. "Since we met, I've thought that the way Brad has lived his life was good and exemplary." She wanted to add "until this past week," but she knew this was not for MacGregor's ears. "But it has always been his narrow-minded beliefs that made me think he was like those uneducated extremists in Baton Rouge. It just didn't fit, and I guess it still doesn't. He is so smart, so educated, and yet he lives in the nineteenth century when it comes to religion."

"Oh, I suspect Brad's faith is a lot older than that." MacGregor smiled slyly.

"Jarrod, though. Oh my. Where do I begin? He has always struck me as a lot more loving and maybe even a lot better at *being* a Christian than Brad, but his beliefs and his church are so strange. In college Jarrod repeatedly told us his account about how 'getting saved' at this crazy church had made him the loving person he is. So I couldn't judge him too harshly. Still, it was a little weird."

"It's a charismatic church, is what she's trying to say," explained Jarrod.

"Whatever," Lauren laughed. "I know. They have taught me a few vocabulary words from their debates, so now I know what words like *charismatic* mean when they talk about it.

"Anyway, Brad and Jarrod have gone round and round about whether charismatic churches are in line with the Bible and whether Southern Baptist churches are dead. At first I thought it a silly and pathetic argument that proved how useless Christianity is, but over time I have come to see them both moderate their views with respect to each other and also come to see how some of the issues at stake have importance. I am normally silent or I play devil's advocate when the charismatic-versus-Baptist issue arises. Thankfully, it only comes up occasionally."

For his part, Jarrod had no illusions that his church and faith were normal. He explained to MacGregor that he knew his church was abnormal but that he reveled in it. Brad's way of being a Christian was at least on the path toward deadness, if not actually dead, in Jarrod's eyes.

"You mean the church I preached in this morning?" asked MacGregor.

"Oh yeah." Jarrod's exclamation hung in the air. The cool, unflappable one realized he was caught. "I didn't mean . . ."

MacGregor let him off the hook. "Don't worry, I'm having fun. Who knows, maybe my sermon deadened things a bit today. I don't mind." He paused and then said, "But you might be careful about painting your brothers and sisters with a broad brush of deadness." He raised his eyebrows as if to say, "OK?"

Jarrod nodded and smiled. "Point taken. And I can honestly say something positive here. Brad will agree that I've often acknowledged that his remarkable character and integrity are truly based on his knowledge of Scripture. That's all good. However, recent events call this into question." He grinned conspiratorially at Brad and Lauren, and Brad reddened and shook his head slightly.

MacGregor surveyed the range of countenances. "Brad, do you need me to hear your confession?"

Lauren laughed out loud. "You have no idea. I didn't know Protestants heard confession, but he definitely needs it."

"You are relentless. Good grief! I've already apologized." Brad turned to the professor. "I don't know if it's really appropriate to get into all this now. Jarrod, can you just get back to what you were saying?"

"Sure. Sorry, Brad, we're just hazing you. All right, back to what I was saying. Look, I respect the Bible, and I know it's important and all, but what I am really all about is the Spirit. That's where there is freedom and life. It's not a bunch of rigid rules and dry-as-dust doctrine. I'm talking real people. Real life. Real power for living."

"Professor, he *means* it," Lauren chuckled. "His church here in Houston is even called Spirit's Power, and I think I've already said it's *wild.*"

"Doesn't matter what week you choose to visit or how many different times you visit, the topic *du jour* is always the same: the Holy Spirit," Brad chipped in.

"Fine. We do talk about the Spirit every week, and you know what, we see amazing things happen. Does anything happen in your church? I don't think so."

Lauren interrupted. "Listen, I'm going to excuse myself to the rest room while you two have your little debate." She nodded to MacGregor and pushed herself away from the table.

Brad and Jarrod watched her walk away, but then, instead of re-engaging their old debate, they communicated their thoughts about Lauren to Professor MacGregor. Jarrod said he felt more need to bring up problems with Brad and his approach to Christianity than he did with Lauren and her beliefs. Brad, for his part, was torn: after years of church and Sunday school and youth camps, he felt compelled to show Jarrod from the Bible just how wrong he was. But he also believed that Jarrod was a Christian, even if he was one of those charismatic Christians, and Lauren was definitely not. Brad said he loved Lauren and respected her mind a great deal. In fact, Brad was frustrated that he lacked the ability to prove to her that the Bible was true and that Jesus was Savior and Lord. For all her intelligence and her sharp reasoning ability, when it came to religion, she seemed merely to default to whatever mainstream culture believed. He knew something had happened in her past but wasn't sure what. All he and Jarrod knew was that whatever had happened made her leave the Catholic Church and become extremely wary of intense Christians. They brought this to a close as Lauren returned from the rest room.

As Lauren sat down, she said, "Hey, you're hearing a lot about us. How about you?"

Jarrod and Brad perked up and Jarrod said, "Yea, what's your story?"

MacGregor replied, "Well, it's a long story but I'll give you the Cliff Notes. I grew up in Houston, went to Princeton for undergrad, where I studied history. I came back to Texas, and Lauren, like you I went to UT Law."

"Really?! That's great."

"I practiced law for several years in Houston, but the Lord was doing a lot of things in my life, including introducing me to my wife, Marilynn. We went off to seminary, and then I earned my Ph.D. in theology. Of course I'm skipping so much—so many years, and all the stories about the children—but eventually after many twists and turns, I came back to Houston to teach at the seminary. I just retired officially a few years ago, but I still teach a class or two each semester. That's me."

"I would love to hear more about what you teach," said Brad.

"And I've got to hear how you went from being an attorney to being a seminary professor," said Lauren.

"Sure. I suspect in time we'll get to all of that. But, I've got a question—so is this what you talk about when you get together here on Sundays?" asked MacGregor.

Brad considered the question for a moment. "Over the years we have had debates over religion as well as discussions about philosophy and politics, but recently the religious topics have arisen less and less."

"That's true," said Lauren. "We're now six years removed from undergrad, so it's natural for our Sunday evening discussions to become more mature."

"Mature?" asked MacGregor.

"You know . . . our talks now have more to do with what's happening in our careers, what we and our friends are doing for fun in our rare moments away from work. And movies . . . we all love movies, and though we hardly have time to see many anymore, we do enjoy dissecting the few that we catch. The religion thing just comes up a lot less. I kind of like it that way," Lauren finished with firmness.

"Not last year. You wanted to press us like crazy about September 11. You kept sticking it to us, or at least to me, last year."

"That's true, but that's just because I was so shaken by all that senseless suffering. I figured if what the Christian extremists always spout were true, then God would never have allowed it."

"Anyway," Brad turned to the professor, "we talk about any and everything in our lives and have done so ever since living in the honors dorm freshman year. And yes, we do talk about religion a fair amount, or we used to, but other things just seem to occupy our Sunday evenings these days."

"This is truly special," said MacGregor with enthusiasm tinged with wonder. "I love this sort of thing myself. Unfortunately I have to get home. Marilynn, my wife, needs me to do some chores tonight, so I need to leave. I guess I want to know whether you want to explore some religious topics further, and whether it's OK if I'm a part of it with you. I really have enjoyed getting to know you, and Brad said you have great discussions, so I'd like to be a part if you don't mind. But I am sensitive to the fact that this is your special time and you are all incredibly busy. I don't want to impose at all."

"I would love to have you join us when you can, at least for awhile, specifically so we can chase some of these religious questions. Lauren's right—we have been talking about this stuff a lot less, and I'm also realizing that I need to focus more on my faith. I'd love for us to do this." Brad staked out his ground.

Jarrod agreed. "It's all good by me. I love this stuff."

Lauren sighed. "I don't know. I kind of liked getting away from the religious topics that we did so much over the years. But I am kind of intrigued about what a professor with a Ph.D. thinks about these things. On the other hand, just recently Brad has made me pretty angry about Christianity again. We really can't go into it because it's personal, but I'm honestly feeling a little hostile to your Christian faith."

"Fair enough," said MacGregor. "Obviously, I don't know what's transpired between you recently, but there are plenty of reasons to be angry at Christians regarding how we live out what we say we believe. Maybe I can help address some of your questions, Lauren."

She smiled. "Maybe, Professor. OK, I'm game. At least for awhile. But I warn you, I'm not going to back down in my skepticism. I'm going to press my questions full force."

"That's fine with me," said MacGregor cheerily. "So shall we meet back in two weeks? Is that the plan?"

"That's the plan," said Jarrod, and the others nodded. This was going to be an interesting fall.

Chapter 3

God in Hitler

BRAD ASSUMED THE ROLE of unofficial coordinator for getting every-one together again, which made perverse sense since he had to break the engagement three weeks running. Though Brad didn't want to miss anything with MacGregor, he finally suggested that they revert to their usual pattern. He E-mailed Lauren and Jarrod:

> You two should meet with MacGregor at Common Grounds this Sunday, and I'll make it if I can. No more postponing the pro-fessor. If I miss, it's my loss. I am making every effort to get there. With the capital markets so slow, the VPs and directors have us doing an absurd amount of due diligence trying to scare up *any* business. Check with you later and hope to see you Sunday.

> Brad

> P.S. Lauren, I hope you're not still mad. I am truly sorry for what happened last month.

† † †

Common Grounds bustled at seven that Sunday evening. The Houston heat and humidity still hung in the air, and though late September generally occasioned the first respite of fall coolness, it was still a bit sticky to sit outside. Lauren arrived early in Capri pants and a sweater draped and tied around her tanned shoulders, her usual picture of understated elegance. Jarrod had never experienced much pressure at Compaq to assume anything close to elegance—khakis and golf shirts were the norm for the programming geeks—but grad school had liberated him to his preferred casual. In deference to the professor, though, Jarrod dressed up—jeans and some raggedly rough woven shirt that exuded a vague hint of '60s authenticity and a pair of abused hemp sandals. His blond hair had not suffered the indignity of scissors in two months, so the old surfer chic was coming in. On Jarrod the unruly locks and clothes-by-the-pound looked completely natural. It was the six years of the generic suburban golf wannabe look at Compaq that had been affected.

MacGregor strolled in right on time, but this time Lauren and Jarrod spied the evidence of a bow tie stuffed in his blazer pocket. Jarrod commented to Lauren as MacGregor came through the door, "I just think it's so funny that he loses the tie to come hang out here."

Lauren chuckled, "Yeah, but I guess he's trying to relate. I think it's sweet."

MacGregor extended his hand first to Lauren and said, "Lauren, so good to see you again. It seems like a long time ago that we were last here." Then he shook Jarrod's hand and winked. "I missed you folks. I was starting to think we were never going to be able to meet."

"Blame Above Average Brad," replied Jarrod. "Or really his bosses. They keep the boy on a short leash. But you never know, he may make it. He usually makes it here every two or three times we meet."

After they ordered their drinks, Lauren and Jarrod led the professor back to their usual table in the corner. They chatted lightly about what they had done the last three weeks. Lauren, choosing to disclose only work-related stuff, edited out the renewed energy she had pumped into her bars and clubs in reaction to Brad's rejection. She had rediscovered the fun of being a total catch in the young social scene downtown, and she had also rediscovered the not quite fulfilling results of all that energy expended on those guys. She knew that Jarrod would shrug if he knew any more than he did, but she felt the need to hide all this from MacGregor.

Jarrod's reading for his moral philosophy course got the conversation out of the light chat mode because MacGregor knew the material backward and forward. Just as they were really getting into things, Brad showed up.

"You made it!" boomed MacGregor heartily. "I'm so glad you're here."

Brad smiled broadly and said, "I get such a different reception at work. But I need a java fix in a bad, bad way. I'll be right back." He snagged some coffee and returned. "All right, what are you all talking about?"

"We've really just been chatting and catching up, though Jarrod was about to get a personal tutorial on Kant's categorical imperative."

"I used to know what that meant," Brad replied with a grin.

"Before you went over to the Dark Side and stopped using your brain," said Jarrod. He winked at the professor. "Clang, clang, round one is starting with a flurry."

Brad laughed. "Bring it on! I'm predicting a TKO in round five. You just keep up the feeble jabs." Turning to MacGregor, he asked, "So, what's on the docket tonight? I can't stay too long. I've got to get back in an hour or so."

"It's not up to me, Brad. I'm just here to spend time with you-all and be a part of your discussion. I'm up for anything. From the way your introductions went when we first met, it's clear that you have a lot of questions and issues you have been debating for years."

"Which issues seemed like the most important?" asked Lauren.

Jarrod jumped in. "Lauren thinks Brad and I are weird because we're Christians who take our faith seriously. So we've tried to convince her that Christianity's true. That's a lot of it. Lauren, the attorney, asks a lot of tough questions trying to undermine us, and Brad and I simply try to survive the onslaught." Brad nodded with a wry expression.

Lauren felt defensive. "Professor, it's not that I don't believe in God. I just don't believe he's like what *they* say about him."

"That sounds like an *excellent* subject to discuss," said the professor. "Why don't we discuss our understandings of who God is? Does that sound all right to you?"

They each nodded.

"Lauren, if you don't mind, why don't you begin? What is your god like?" asked the professor.

"Sure, I'd be happy to. For starters, he's very tolerant. He loves *all* people, not just church people. He's there when you need him. He doesn't have to control everyone. We definitely do our own thing." Lauren's words were firm, but she spoke in a pleasant tone. "Oh, and everybody is OK with him. In other words, he's not sending people to hell just because they have different perspectives. As Deepak Chopra says, 'God is loving light, bathing all in the warmth of his love.' He lets us make mistakes, and he doesn't get angry but just helps us to learn from our mistakes."

"Does he give guidance?" MacGregor inquired.

"Sure. Just think about your problem or situation, and you get this sense, and you know what you're supposed to do. This happens for me daily in my work. I mostly work with the same few partners, but the client roster for those partners is pretty long. Even though things have been slower at work with the economic downturn, I still have a stack of active files that all need attention. And you know the pressure to bill hours. So as clients call in or E-mail, I can be overwhelmed with the amount of detailed work that I have to perform. Knowing which file to work on—down to which task to do—can be overwhelming when so much else has to be done at the same time.

"So I take a deep breath or two, and then I just think about what I should be doing. Sometimes immediately or sometimes after a few minutes, I get a little sense of guidance or solution. I think that's God."

"When you follow his guidance, does it ever result in one of those mistakes you mentioned?"

"No, of course not."

MacGregor sat still, silent, with an understanding expression on his face. Jarrod shook his head and grinned, and Brad cleared his throat demonstratively. Lauren's lips pressed thinly together, and she flashed them a minor glare.

Lauren had a choice, to treat this like a Rambo deposition that her litigator friends talked about and contest everything MacGregor asked or stated, or she could dial down a bit of her adversarial training and instead treat this like a normal conversation. Christians usually tempted her to be difficult, but there was something about the professor that took a little of the edge off. She was used to being in the driver's seat, or at least a position of parity, in most conversations and giving ground to this stranger didn't come easily. She felt strangely and consciously aware of a flare-up of indignation at being challenged so casually by this person she had only recently met, but she also became consciously aware that the indignation was rapidly followed by an instinct to trust this old man. *Let it go,* an inner voice urged. She sighed and decided to go the normal conversation route. That meant being honest. She sighed again and finally relented. "I guess sometimes I make mistakes."

"I'm not talking about just making mistakes. Especially about which file or client to focus on, though these practical concerns are important. I'm talking about making mistakes about any matter *after* you have received the sense of guidance that you say is God."

She thought for a moment. He was good. In an instant she saw several possible lines of argument and where they were headed. It would be easier to hijack this before she got put on the defensive. But he had made a good point, and it was an honest question about what she really believed. Besides, she was confident about what she'd always believed.

"Yes, there have been times when bad results occurred when I followed that sense of guidance."

"So . . . does your god just not know how to guide you, or does he know and just purposefully lead you into mistakes?"

"I suppose the former. He just doesn't know. He wouldn't lead me into harm on purpose."

MacGregor smiled. "OK, I think I'm coming to understand him a little better. Now please forgive me. As Brad said, I teach theology at the seminary. We theologians have this annoying habit of making distinctions and creating categories with fancy jargon. If I were to distill the substance of what you just said into 'formal attributes' "—MacGregor used his hands to imitate quotation signs—"of God, you would say he is sometimes ignorant but that he is righteous."

"What do you mean by *righteous?*"

"By righteous I mean morally pure. He does right. He wouldn't lead you astray because his character is good. He does good, not evil."

"Yes, that part's true, but I don't like what you said before that about him being ignorant. That makes him sound stupid or uneducated. But yes, he is definitely righteous. He wouldn't harm people intentionally."

"Lauren, I want to be careful here. I take what you're saying seriously, and I'm honored that you will tell me about your beliefs that are so personal to you. If I'm not careful, I risk offending you. Many people can be offended when other people ask questions about their religious beliefs. It's normal to feel somewhat attacked when the subject is religion and your beliefs are on the line. But I don't want to attack you; I really just want to understand. Will you give me permission to ask questions to clarify for my own understanding?"

"Of course. I'm glad that you want to listen and to know more of what I think. Usually these two"—she tilted her head in the direction of Brad and Jarrod—"just preach 'the truth' at me, and I fire away with questions."

"But, Lauren, this is where I have to be careful, and this is why I'm asking your permission. For me to understand, I have to ask clarifying questions. And I fear that some of these questions will arise because

I might hear what *sounds* like inconsistency. Now I realize you're an attorney, so this is normal to you, except that we're not talking about your professional life or something distant. We're talking about you and your core beliefs. It's different. What might be fine in a professional context can be really offensive in a personal context. I don't want to offend you or press you. So I want to know if you're OK with my asking about things that appear inconsistent."

Lauren thought for a second. Yes, she hated when people pointed out flaws in her reasoning. She was usually right, and her reputation for being smart and being right ensured that things often went her way. But it just made the times she was wrong all the more painful; her pride got in the way. But what was she going to say, no? This man was so gracious and careful, how could she tell him, "No, you can't ask hard questions"? She looked at MacGregor again and felt the same feeling as before—kind, accepting, sweet.

"Yes, I suppose," she replied resignedly. "I mean, who likes to have holes in your thinking exposed? But I can't really say no."

"Actually, you can," urged MacGregor. "Otherwise this whole thing is uncomfortable for you. It's your call whether you want to share information and take questions about your most personal beliefs. We can change the subject, talk about news, sports, movies. I will—*we* will—respect your decision. You're not under pressure to continue this."

"No, no. It's OK. I really *should* be consistent."

"Well, Lauren, you say that God can lead you into mistakes, but you take exception to his having the attribute of ignorance. Ignorance is literally the 'lack of knowledge' about a particular thing. If God doesn't know something, then he is, at least with respect to that something, ignorant. Your god may know many things, even most things. He may know everything except one or two things. But technically speaking, about those one or two things, he is ignorant."

"But I don't want to say that *God* is ignorant. That sounds awful."

"I understand that you don't want to ascribe ignorance to God. But if he *is* unaware of some things, including giving you guidance so faulty that it leads you into a mistake, how is that *not* ignorance?"

"You don't see how that is rude? I'm really surprised. You just don't say things like that about people you care about. You especially don't say things like that about God!"

"Lauren, I understand that we don't like attributing unpopular or unpleasant characteristics to people to whom we are close. But it comes down to what is *real.* Your stance is about being loyal to a person, and my stance is about being loyal to the truth. If I may put it baldly, I contend that loyalty to truth trumps loyalty to a fallible person. Granted, most of the time my loyalties to people concur with loyalty to truth, but where people fall short of truth, I stay loyal to truth."

"That's a recipe for loneliness. Who wants to be friends with someone who is all truth? Besides, one thing I've learned from the study of law is that truth is elusive, if it even exists. I want to say it exists, but it seems that no one can agree on what it is."

"Hmm, interesting that you say that. Truth *is* elusive for mere humans to grasp." This statement raised the eyebrows of Brad, but Jarrod nodded. "But my own experience in knowing the truth has been that it sets me free. I've come to follow the truth and get to know the truth better and better. Truth is my friend; I'm not alone at all." He spoke easily, humbly.

Brad jumped in. "I agree. In my business you have some folks who kiss up to guys more senior, who say whatever they think the VP or director wants to hear. We spin numbers a fair amount, trying to get the analysis to look right to get a client to bite on the deal. But there are limits. You can't outright lie, and even though we all know we're engaging in spin or presentation of a particular lens of the company's work, ultimately we are pitching our due diligence to the client who has a decent sense of what his company is worth. You can't just make stuff up. Occasionally you hear through the grapevine about an overly aggressive VP or director who stretched things in pitch. But bending facts in order to ingratiate yourself with the client gets you a reputation. You're respected if people know you shoot straight. Truth matters, even if it gets spun a little in the packaging."

MacGregor looked at Lauren to see if this was connecting at all. She seemed wary but open.

"Lauren, tying this back to what you said about your god—loyalty to what is real means saying that your god doesn't know certain things and thus he is ignorant. Does that make sense?"

Lauren nodded. "Yes, it does. But at least he is, as you say, righteous. He isn't malicious."

"Good. So we actually have several attributes of your god so far. He is loving because you said he loves all people. He is tolerant. He is ignorant about some things, and he is righteous. So far so good?"

Lauren nodded affirmatively but then looked at him quizzically. She had never heard anyone take inventory of God's attributes before. It wasn't bad. It was actually interesting and helpful. It was just unlike anything she had ever heard.

"Now earlier you said he does not control. So does your god have any power?"

Still wary, she replied, "I want to say he does, but . . ."

"Is there anything or anyone more powerful than he? Are there things that are technically doable but that he cannot do?"

"No. I can't think of anything more powerful than God."

"How about humans? Are humans more powerful than God?"

"Why no! Why do you ask that? Isn't that kind of silly?" Again Lauren looked at him quizzically.

"Yes, I suppose it is silly to suggest that humans are more powerful than God." MacGregor smiled. "But I thought you said your god was not in control. Didn't you say humans are in control of their own lives?"

"Yes, we are."

"So are not humans more powerful than your god? He's not in control; we are. We have more power than he does."

Lauren grimaced at hearing her own words come back at her. This was so frustrating! She knew where this was going. If she said God was more powerful than people, then he would be in control, and that would contradict what she said earlier. If, to stay consistent, she said humans are in control, then she would be contradicting her recent statement moments ago about God being more powerful than humans.

"OK, I see the problem. I *want* to believe them both. You know Barry Zuchoff, the spiritual advisor to the celebrities? He says, 'Oneness is God, and God's oneness is us.' Therefore, maybe these concepts *can* go together. When I talk about God, I want to say he is powerful and more powerful than humans. When I talk about humans, I want to talk about our freedom to do anything and be in control of our lives."

"Yes," said MacGregor, "but when you put them together—when God intersects with humans—you've got that problem you said you see. Either God is in control, or humans are. Or you have a contradiction. I imagine in your line of work that you make short work of people who express contradictions. Do you have a sort of standard retort when you're deposing someone and he or she tries to defend contradictory statements?"

Lauren smiled at realizing the professor was aware of a lawyer's deposition tactics. "Yes, I do, in fact." She looked at Brad and Jarrod in a manner expressing that MacGregor had her again. She shook her head. "I don't really do depositions myself. Corporate law doesn't have me doing that sort of thing. But I know what litigators say. They usually say something about how the contradiction of the deponent makes his or her statement *nonsensical*."

The professor paused. He didn't want to make this unpleasant. He could see the point was made without pressing the problem of her contradiction further.

"Let's move to something else. Where is your god?"

"*Where?* Oh, I don't know. I guess he's everywhere. He's in every-thing and everybody. He's in you and me. I know it's a cliché, but it's true. There's a spark of God in each one of us."

"OK. This is good. I'm getting to know your god better and better. Another question: Does evil exist?"

"Of course it does. Take Hitler, for example."

"Is God in Hitler?"

"No. God is not in Hitler. OK, God is not in *everybody.* But he's in most people." Lauren grinned because she owned up to the inconsis-tency before MacGregor could ask her about it.

MacGregor returned the grin. "OK. Fair enough. But I've got a question about all this: How do you *know* this information about God?"

This was a stumper. Jarrod and Brad, who had watched with rapt attention as the professor explored Lauren's god, looked at him afresh. Yeah, how *did* she know all this stuff about God?

Lauren felt stumped herself. She knew an answer, and it was her answer that she really believed. But she also knew that it was inade-quate and that she was about to see her answer pulled apart.

"I just do. Look, I know this is different from the way you justify things in school and from the way you justify things in law. But my answer to your question is, I *feel* it. And I see this in my life a lot. My friends, at least the ones who believe in God, think as I do. I've never really studied it, but I just know this is what I believe and what most people believe. I mean, when I watch TV, when I see movies, I occasionally see references to God, and this is what we all believe. I'm not alone. This is pretty stan-dard stuff." She was warming up again. "In fact, the *only* time I really feel uncomfortable with religious talk or when I hear about God is when extremist Christians are in the news or when I run into them or hear their closed-minded views." She paused. "So I guess that's how I know, and even though it's not strong, well-reasoned knowledge, I feel OK with how I know because just about everyone else in society seems to know the same things about God for the same reasons. We just feel it."

"But in terms of a specific source of your information about your god, you can't identify one?" asked MacGregor.

"No. But that doesn't make it any less true."

"OK. It's interesting that you say that. That leads to another question: How do you know what is true?"

How do I know what is true? Lauren repeated to herself. *What my mom taught me. What teachers in school taught me. What my friends say.* Aloud she said, "Lots of ways—family, school, reading, peers."

"Do they ever say conflicting things? When what your family believes conflicts with what a peer says, how do you determine which is right or if neither is right?"

"I just go with what I feel is best."

"OK. Another question: How do you know Hitler was evil? What makes something evil, and what makes something good? Where do you get your standard for measuring some things as evil and others as good?"

Lauren replied immediately. "Same as before. Family, school, peers."

"So if the Germans of Hitler's time said, 'Hey, Jews are bad. They are subhuman. They are greedy backstabbers who made us lose World War I. Go ahead, exterminate them,' then that's OK with you?"

"Of course that's not OK! It is the greatest evil in history!" Lauren's face flashed with anger.

"But you said you learned evil from what you were taught by family, school, and peers. So did the Germans. Many Germans of that era grew up in an environment of anti-Semitism. Being anti-Jewish was a fairly normal thing. They learned evil and good the same way you did, but they came up with different conclusions. We return to the question, Where do you get your standard by which to measure evil and good?"

"I don't know. All I have is what I've been taught and what I feel."

"But you see, if everyone goes by what they've been taught, African-Americans might still be slaves or at least deprived of civil rights.

Surely you don't think something is right or good just because it was taught to them."

"I don't. But why are you asking me these questions about truth and evil? I thought we were talking about what God is like?"

"We are. But a crucial question is, What is the source of the information we have? We get erroneous information regularly about financial investments, which sports team performs better, which traffic route is quickest, which business model is most efficient, which factors are key in dating relationships. Don't you experience this?"

"Obviously I get bad information about men. Look who I hang out with." She flashed an impish look toward Jarrod and Brad, who simulated glares back at her.

"Lauren," continued the professor patiently, "likewise, we can have erroneous information about God and what he is like. That's why it's crucial to have a good source for truth, for a standard to measure good and evil."

"OK, what's your source? The Bible? The Bible is an ancient book of myths and contradictions. Educated people just don't believe it anymore. One of my professors in college just mocked it throughout his whole religion class. It's like a fairy tale with some common-sense wisdom thrown in."

Jarrod and Brad took umbrage at Lauren's cavalier criticism of their faith. But MacGregor was guiding the conversation, and a look from him told them to refrain from comment.

"Lauren, tell you what. I propose an investigation. You have been kind enough to tell us about your god and where you got your information about him. I don't think we're done, but you've given us a good bit of information this evening. I suspect if we keep meeting in months to come, you're going to tell us a whole lot more about your god. And I welcome it. I really want to take you seriously and understand you and what you believe.

"I would also like to invite you to investigate our God. In other words, allow us to tell you about the God we worship, what his attributes are, what he's like. Just as you shared with us, we will share with you. The point is that we're not going to shove anything down your throat. It'll be like telling you about someone we know and really admire. How does that sound?"

"It sounds fine except for one thing. I mean, I am actually interested, especially since you were asking all those questions about the 'attributes,' as you call them. But I know your source of information about him, and I just don't think much of the Bible. I already told you that I think it's like Greek mythology and fairy tales. Since that's what the Bible is—at least in my opinion—isn't it just a waste of time to tell me about the God of the Bible?"

"Maybe," MacGregor shrugged. "I'm certainly not trying to prove anything to you or prove you wrong. I just thought as a matter of cultural or theological or intellectual interest that you might want to hear our story. I realize you've heard aspects of Christianity before, but perhaps you've not heard it as our story before."

Brad and Jarrod both looked puzzled and exchanged glances. Neither had heard talk like this from Christians, let alone a Christian leader.

"That's fine. But I already know at least one thing about your God. He's awfully uptight about his followers dating people with different beliefs." She mostly managed the line matter-of-factly, but a trace of anger adhered to her words.

MacGregor looked puzzled, but then he saw Lauren shoot a look at Brad. Brad broke eye contact and reached for his cup of coffee. Jarrod looked around and shook his head. Tension that had built a bit with Lauren's uncharitable characterizations of the Bible now mounted considerably.

"Look, I am not nosy, and I don't need to hear anything private between you. But something is impinging on your friendship, and I think it's affecting our ability to have a free, open, and honest conversation about important matters." MacGregor engaged the strangeness head-on.

Brad exhaled demonstrably. "Professor, I might as well tell you, because you're right, there is a huge subtext going on. I screwed up big a month ago. I guess, from time to time over the years, Lauren and I have had little flare-ups of attraction. We never really talked about it, but we both sensed these occasional flare-ups. But almost every time, if I was feeling attracted, she wasn't and vice versa. And on the whole, this has not been a major factor in our friendship.

"Then a month ago, I was tired but jacked up from a deal that had gone well. It was a bad combination. Lauren was having her own mixed feelings about life and work. And this time we both zigged or zagged together. The attraction was there for both of us."

"You're leaving something out," said Jarrod dryly.

Brad exhaled again. "Jarrod and I have talked about this before." Brad had to be careful because he couldn't 'out' Jarrod—the fact that Jarrod, too, occasionally was interested in Lauren. "Because I am a Christian, and Lauren's not, it's really not appropriate for me to let things go this direction. So starting back at UT, I've never acted on those flare-ups because I knew nothing could ever come of it."

"But he did last month," said Lauren vehemently. "We met up and talked, and we ended up kissing. I thought it was wonderful. I was all excited. Then the next day he calls me feeling all guilty and says it was a mistake because I'm not a Christian. And because we're all friends together, Brad had to tell Jarrod about it. Not only did it make everything awkward for us as a group, but also it made me furious that Brad can be so narrow-minded and judgmental. I cannot believe that you Christians are so arrogant as to think you can't date people with different beliefs. It's all the same God, anyway. You are just supporting bigotry. I can't believe educated people can actually be this way."

MacGregor blinked slowly and purposefully and eyed Brad with an expression of sympathy for a guy getting caught being a guy. "You've got a lot of 'splaining to do." Then he looked back at Lauren. "Lauren, I am truly sorry. It makes perfect sense that you feel judged and cheated out of something good. You're angry for legitimate reasons. I am genuinely sorry that you were hurt."

"So you agree with me? I thought you were going to take their side on this, that Christians should be all closed-minded and not date or marry people from other religions." MacGregor's expression of support didn't take the edge off her vehemence even slightly. She had her eye on the ball and was swinging for the fences.

The professor glanced around, noticing both the tension and the empty cups.

"That's a tough question. I don't really want to focus on inter-religious dating right now, but I will in the future if we keep meeting together and you all want to talk about this question. But let's try something. There's already a fair amount of tension at this table about our views of God and the Bible. Tell you what, why don't we take a moment to refill our glasses or run to the rest room. Lauren, at the end I will *briefly* take a stab at your question about Christians dating non-Christians because you are legitimately upset about it. But let's agree to postpone a full discussion on that for some other time. Let's first finish what we started, which was discussing the characteristics of your god and the Christian God. When we return to the table, can we start over fresh with the Christian picture of God? If we have time, I'll say a few words about the dating question. Sound good?"

They all agreed, and their shoulders relaxed slightly, suggesting that MacGregor's attempt to de-escalate worked a little. Their chairs scraped the wood floor as they stood up, collected their cups and glasses, and headed to the counter for fill-ups. Brad wondered if round two would be any less intense.

Chapter 4

The Grand Canyon

RECONVENED A FEW MINUTES LATER, they were bantering about their java proclivities and the pluses and minuses of different coffee beans. Their moods had brightened considerably, and MacGregor segued back into the discussion.

"Lauren, I hear your concerns about Scripture. That's fine. You're not the first, and you're not likely to be the last to have objections to the Bible. But tell you what: How about if you let us share a little bit about our God, tell you what he's like, and we'll deal with this whole issue of the Bible's authority some other time? For now, just consider our discussion one of getting to know the God of a particular story. We're inviting you to hear our story. We're not trying to prove anything to you, just tell you our story. What do you say?"

"That's fine. In a way I can suspend my disbelief and look at this as getting to know the character of a story." Her prior rancor about intolerant Christians and their hopelessly out-of-date Bible subsided significantly. *This could be interesting,* she thought. "Go for it."

"Thank you. Now, crusty professional theologians like myself for centuries have identified the attributes of God found in Scripture. We do need to proceed with caution because if we're not careful, you'll get the idea that this is all so much distant abstraction. God is not an abstraction. He is a living person who creates, mourns, romances, and delights. Scholastic theologians can do a number on Scripture and torture the verses into abstractions on a page that barely resemble the exuberantly alive God that he reveals himself to be.

"Having said that, it is still useful to get to know this living God in part by learning his character. Some of the attributes have fancy Latin names, and the list is somewhat long. We could talk about twenty or so attributes of God found in Scripture, but I think that's a bit much for a coffee-shop chat. So we'll just touch on a few of the attributes of our God. Jarrod, why don't you lead us off. Who is your God? Tell us one thing about him."

Jarrod relished the opportunity to respond to Lauren's knocking of Christianity. While he had never gotten into the Bible much, his charismatic church imbued a strong loyalty to Christ; and since UT days, he loved philosophy of religion. "I'd say he is truth. I liked it when Professor MacGregor said he's not alone when he's loyal to truth because truth is his friend. God says he himself is the truth."

"Of course God is the truth. But he is the same truth of all religions," replied Lauren.

"No, I don't mean it that way. I don't know *where* God said it, but I know that he did. Professor, do you know the passage I'm talking about? And by chance did you bring your Bible?"

"Always. Professional tool of my trade." MacGregor reached inside his blazer and pulled out a slender, worn leather Bible. "I believe you're thinking of this passage." The professor thumbed through a few pages before turning it around for Jarrod and Lauren to read.

Lauren spied where the professor's finger marked a verse and she began, "He says, 'I am the way and the truth and the life. No one comes to the Father except through me.' So that's his own description of himself—the truth."

That's strange, thought Lauren. "Jesus described himself as *the* truth?" she asked skeptically. "I know Brad and Jarrod have said their religion is the truth for years, and coming from Louisiana, I'm used to a lot of people thinking that Christianity is the truth, but I never thought Jesus would say such a thing."

Lauren noted the verse—John 14:6—and read it several times. Who would have thought that someone as enlightened as Jesus would say something so intolerant? She was surprised. Even though she didn't believe in the Bible, she had always thought of Jesus as one of the great prophets or spiritual gurus like the Buddha and Gandhi. Either he was not as enlightened as she thought, or she had some rethinking to do about intolerance.

MacGregor looked at Brad and nodded.

Brad said, "OK, I guess it's my turn. *Our* God is not ignorant." He winked at Lauren. "Our God is the opposite; he's omniscient." Lauren nodded. "*Omniscience* means 'knowing all things.' God knows everything. He knows the past, he knows the present, and he knows the future."

Lauren interrupted, "Brad, I know what *omniscience* means. We've talked about the issue before. You know, does God know everything, and if he does, how does free will work in with that? Don't you remember that big debate we had back in college when Jarrod was writing that paper about free will and determinism?"

"Of course I remember. But I'd like to show you the scriptural basis for Christians believing that God is omniscient." Brad reached for the professor's Bible and flipped the pages until he arrived at Psalm 139. "Please read here, through verse 4."

Lauren read aloud, "O LORD, you have searched me and you know me. You know when I sit and when I rise; you perceive my thoughts from afar. You discern my going out and my lying down; you are familiar with all my ways. Before a word is on my tongue you know it completely, O LORD." A pleasant sensation flooded Lauren. She read it again, this time to herself.

Brad started to explain, "Now I know this can sound really frightening, like Big Brother and—"

"No, not at all. I like this. This is good. I don't get Big Brother out of this at all. In fact, it makes me think of love."

Jarrod's and Brad's eyebrows rose, but MacGregor just smiled. She continued. "OK, I know that sounds strange. But when you think about it, it's really not that strange at all. My girlfriends and I talk about how we hate the fact that most of the guys we date don't communicate that well. We start going out with some guy, and he's handsome and all and usually pretty athletic. Everything's great at first, but then they don't *talk.* They don't tell me what's going on in their lives. It's amazing; in a bar they are so funny and animated and the life of the party, but when we're alone, they just can't *talk.* I try to pull stuff out of them, and they get all hassled. It's frustrating.

"And here's the thing: it's not just that I want to know them deeply. I want them to know me. I want us to know each other. And when they get all aloof, not only are they not allowing me to know them, but also they obviously don't want to know me. When I try sharing something personal, they seem to get distracted, or jumpy, or just irritated, and I end up just feeling used. When I'm with a guy, I really want to know him and have him know me."

Lauren's finger tapped the open Scripture. "So when I read this, that God knows me—I mean *really, really* knows me—that's wonderful. I love it! It makes me want to get to know him. I've never thought this before."

You could have heard a pin drop after that. After a few moments a broadly smiling Jarrod reached toward Lauren to touch fists, a version of the high five that Jarrod brought from the world of wakeboarding and a gesture the two often shared.

"I love it too. You're catching the idea of how cool God is and the fun of hanging out with God."

"The idea of hanging out with a cool God pretty much dominates Jarrod's understanding of God," Brad said good-naturedly. Brad could tell that Jarrod delighted that he and Lauren for the first time seemed to be tracking on the whole God thing.

Lauren's comments, however, perplexed Brad. He loved Lauren and counted her as one of his best friends. Yet he longed for her to leave behind her worldly lifestyle. She'd always been one to work hard and play hard, and while she had less time these days, Lauren was definitely into the party scene and all that it entailed. Brad couldn't figure out why Lauren would *want* God to know about her behavior. After all, he grew up in the church, believed in Christ, and tried to live a moral life, and even he found the idea that God knew him deeply to be scary. Brad realized his own sin too much to take comfort in the idea of being completely known. *Perhaps ignorance is bliss,* thought Brad. *She doesn't realize what God knows about her.*

MacGregor nodded and simply said, "I'm with you, Lauren. It's an inexpressible comfort to know that God knows me utterly—and still loves me. You see, our God is also a God of love. And when I see his love on one hand and perfect knowledge of me on the other, putting those together makes me want to worship."

Lauren wasn't used to words like *worship* in her everyday vocabulary, but she understood. She was seeing more wisdom in this man than before. He seemed to get her. She nodded.

Brad regained his train of thought. "And part of God's omniscience is that he knows the future, and so he can predict what will happen with perfect accuracy. In fact, a lot of prophecies in the Old Testament were fulfilled hundreds of years later by Jesus. God knew what was going to happen. This is also important because"—his trademark sly smile reappearing—"our God never gives wrong guidance. He would never have to say he's sorry for leading you into a mistake. Omniscience means knowing all things, being supremely wise about all things, and so he leads us in straight paths."

Brad was a bit too triumphal, which was annoying, but Lauren saw for the umpteenth time that he cared about God. It was endearing to see a driven businessman be so into spirituality. But it was time for a question.

"Wait. If God knows the future perfectly, does he know what you're going to do in five minutes? Does he know if you'll get an A on your next paper, Jarrod?"

MacGregor answered, "Good question. One way to begin to answer that question is to say that God's knowledge is related to God's power. In other words, God's omniscience is related to his omnipotence."

Lauren nodded. "*Omnipotence* being the word for 'all-powerful.'"

"Right," continued the professor. "The Scriptures depict God as having the whole world under his control. He can do any *possible* thing. With his 'all power' working hand in glove with 'all knowledge,' God rules and governs the universe wisely. He ultimately works all things for good. So his omniscience and omnipotence converge, and theologians call this the doctrine of Providence."

MacGregor continued. "Lauren, you said that when you think about humans, you think about us as being in control and not God controlling us. If God were not all-powerful but just had *some* power, he would just be 'semi-potent' instead of omnipotent. That might sound nice—like it protects your freedom to do as you please—but it's really scary. It means that there might be situations in which something or someone else can overpower God. It could mean that evil could triumph over him in the end. But this is not the case. Scripture tells us that nothing is impossible for God and that none of his plans can be thwarted. And the overall conclusion is that we can rest secure in him because he knows all and has all power and he is loving. As long as God is on his throne, everything is going to be OK."

Lauren drank all this in. They waited, watching her.

Finally she said, "No questions. At least not until later. I am enjoying this. Tell me more about your God."

The professor gestured to Brad and Jarrod and said, "Take it away."

Brad thought for a moment, and he said, "Actually, something Lauren said earlier about her god being in everything reminded me of another attribute of the Christian God." He turned to Lauren. "And what you said about God knowing you deeply relates well to this. This is his attribute of omnipresence."

Lauren replied, "Ah yes. You mean the idea that he's present all the time or everywhere or something like that."

"Yes. There's a verse right after the passage I just had us read in Psalm 139. I believe it's verses 7 through 10."

"Where can I go from your Spirit? Where can I flee from your presence? If I go up to the heavens, you are there; if I make my bed in the depths, you are there. If I rise on the wings of the dawn, if I settle on the far side of the sea, even there your hand will guide me, your right hand will hold me fast." Lauren looked up, "This is wonderful! I really like this!"

"This is really cool stuff." Jarrod's enthusiasm matched Lauren's. "For me it's the same reason you like the fact that God knows you deeply; it's the fact that he's always there."

MacGregor said, "What is beautiful about this also is that King David, the author, is using a bit of Hebrew poetic style to say something beyond specific places where God is. David is saying that from the heavens to the depths, from east to west—basically everywhere in the world—God is there, and we can behold him. From the highest to the lowest, from one direction to the other, God is there.

"But there is a difference between the God of the Bible and Lauren's God. Our God is not *in* everything and everybody. He's everywhere present, but he's not in the trees, in rocks, and so on. That would be *pantheism*—everything has God in it, and together everything equals God. No, the Christian God is everywhere present, but he's not *in* everything. He is distinct from his creation the way a painter is distinct from his painting. Does that make sense?"

They all nodded. Lauren said, "I could contest that, but I agreed to hear you tell me about your God. What else?"

The professor said, "Well, we've got a good start. We've looked at God's attributes of truth, omniscience, omnipotence, and omnipresence. Jarrod, do you have another one you want to talk about?"

"I wish I knew more of this. We've basically hit the ones I'm most familiar with. That God is love and that Jesus is truth. Maybe Brad knows some more?"

"Sure. I know from talking with a Muslim friend that their deity, Allah, is impersonal. It just seems like fate. But the Christian God is personal. He *is* a person. At times he is joyful, he gets sad, he gets angry. The fact that he has knowledge means he has intelligence. He's a person."

Lauren nodded. "I buy that."

Jarrod said, "Oh, I know another one. It's one that Lauren mentioned earlier. Remember, you said your god is righteous because he wouldn't intentionally lead you into a mistake? Well, the Christian God is righteous too."

"Well said, Jarrod." The professor reached for his Bible and then turned to the Old Testament. "Look at this," he said, pointing at Deuteronomy 32:4. "He is the Rock, his works are perfect, and all his ways are just. A faithful God who does no wrong, upright and just is he.'

"It's important that we understand that God is perfectly righteous, perfectly just, and that is the way he is. He does not conform to some outside standard of what justice is or what doing rightly is. Rather, *he* is the standard. *He* is the measuring rod. His character is perfect, and what he does is the standard for all other beings."

A pause ensued. "OK, how about one more?" asked MacGregor. "We could do so many more—like God's being eternal, invisible, independent. We could talk about mercy and grace. They're all important, of course, but we can only handle so much at one time. To our earlier list we've added 'personal' and 'righteous.' The last one we'll deal with is holiness. Our God is a holy God."

Lauren couldn't resist the cheap pun, but to her it also had cultural relevance. "Holier than thou?"

"You have no idea," replied MacGregor. "In many places in Scripture, God is described as holy. One of my hobbies is committing important quotes and verses from the Bible to memory, and one of my favorites is Psalm 99:1–5: 'The LORD reigns, let the nations tremble; he sits enthroned between the cherubim, let the earth shake. Great is the LORD in Zion; he is exalted over all the nations. Let them praise your great and awesome name—he is holy.'

"'The King is mighty, he loves justice—you have established equity; in Jacob you have done what is just and right. Exalt the LORD our God and worship at his footstool; he is holy.'

"Isn't that wonderful? That one verse encapsulates much of what holiness is."

Lauren understood some of the references. "I know cherubim are angels, and from the Middle East crisis I know that Zion must mean Israel. But what or who is Jacob?"

MacGregor laughed. "Brad, Jarrod, either of you want to answer?"

"Jacob is a reference to the son of Isaac. Abraham was the father of the nation of Israel, and so Jacob was his grandson." Brad paused. "In fact, Jacob the grandson had his name changed *to* Israel. So, when you see 'Jacob,' as in this verse, it is a reference to Israel. And as for Zion, Zion refers to Jerusalem or the mountain on which Jerusalem is built. That's more than two decades of Southern Baptist Sunday school talking," he explained with a grin.

"Well done, Brad. Now what do you think holiness is as you hear that verse?" MacGregor quoted Psalm 99 again.

"I think it has to do with his doing what is just and right," said Brad. "It seems like another way of saying righteousness. I know when I think of holiness, I think of someone who is morally good."

"That's right, Brad. Holiness does mean moral purity, moral perfection. It has to do with the idea that nothing pollutes God or corrupts him. He is utterly good, righteous, clean. But this verse also points to another meaning of *holiness*."

No one said anything, so MacGregor continued. "Did you hear the part about God being enthroned, reigning and exalted above all else?

The other part of holiness is about being 'set apart.' God *transcends* or is *above* us and the world. That is, he is majestic, he is glorious, he is above and beyond us. And guess what happens in Scripture when people encounter God: They fall down and worship! They encounter God, and they realize that he is other than they are, that he is high and lifted up, that he is morally pure and utterly blameless. When they encounter this mysterious, awe-inspiring God, they do the right thing; they fall down and worship."

The old professor stirred them. Brad could feel the awe of God. In their corner of Common Grounds, it seemed like their secret, that God was perforating the normal and touching him. Brad looked at Jarrod and guessed he felt the same inner tug toward gratitude and worship right then and there, just hearing MacGregor's words. Lauren, though, looked uncomfortable.

"Lauren, what's wrong?" asked MacGregor.

"I'm not sure. That just seems terrible and frightening."

"Why? I thought you liked hearing about God knowing you deeply and being everywhere."

"I did, but this is something else. I guess I didn't connect all that with this morality stuff. It's about us being lower than him and his being perfect. That's a little unnerving. It's intimidating. It doesn't seem nice or loving at all."

MacGregor looked down for a moment and then looked back at her. He just looked into her eyes with those kindly eyes of his own. "Lauren, you're absolutely right. It is scary to encounter the holy God. Scripture describes his holiness as a *blinding* light. He is awful in the sense that he fills us with awe. We *should* fear him."

"But you said he was loving."

"He is. But he is also holy. This reminds me of the C. S. Lewis children's stories. Ever read *The Chronicles of Narnia?*"

"Sort of. When I was in fifth grade, my teacher read a book every day at the end of lunch period. She read *The Lion, the Witch and the*

Wardrobe to us, and we were all captivated. She ended up reading two or three more before the school year ended. I don't remember much except that they were magical stories that had us riveted after lunch."

"Well, in that first book, *The Lion, the Witch and the Wardrobe,* little Lucy has stumbled into Narnia, and she is taken in by a family of talking beavers. Mrs. Beaver talks about Aslan in reverent tones, and Lucy asks who Aslan is. The Beavers can't believe she's never heard of the greatest being in their world, and so Mrs. Beaver describes Aslan the lion. And Lucy says, 'A lion? Is he safe?' That's a great question for a little girl. She's hearing about a great lion, and she wants to know if he is safe. Mrs. Beaver's reply is classic: '*Safe?* No, he's not safe; he's a *lion.* But he's good.' And that's how the Lord is: he's a fearsome lion, and he's not safe, but he is good. He is good and loving. It is the most wonderful combination ever."

Lauren appeared unassuaged by the children's story.

MacGregor tried a different tack. "Lauren, the god you believe in— do you worship this god?"

"What do you mean, 'worship'?"

"I mean, do you praise him? Do you tell him how great he is? Do you seek to bring him honor? Do you *love* him?"

"Not really, no. Why?"

"Lauren, I want to say this gently, but perhaps . . . perhaps your god doesn't inspire worship. When people in ancient times and when people today encounter the God of the Bible, they worship. They see that he is an unsafe, blindingly holy lion, and that he is loving and good and merciful. And the combination of his attributes—perfection all together—makes people gasp in wonder or sing in joy or pray with intensity."

The three were caught up in what the professor was saying, so he went on.

"Or how about this? Have you ever been to the Grand Canyon?"

"Yes, once, during college I took a road trip with some friends. It was incredible, probably the greatest thing I've ever seen or experienced."

"And when you stepped up to the edge of the canyon, what did you feel?"

"I felt awe. I was humbled. It was so breathtakingly beautiful and enormous and great, I remember just wanting to cry and shout at the same time. I felt like collapsing on the ground, and I felt like dancing. It was surreal. I couldn't take in all the vastness and all the beauty."

"So what did you do?" MacGregor asked again.

"I said, 'Wow.' My friends and I said wow to each other about a hundred times."

"What else?"

"Well, we started pointing things out, like a beautiful series of lines in the rock or the expanse of cliffs and canyon that we could see for miles. We just said, 'Look at this!' and 'Look at that!' over and over."

"And you couldn't get enough of it, could you?"

"No! It was amazing. I felt so grateful and small, and we were all blown away."

"Lauren, that's worship."

She looked at him again and slowly nodded twice.

"You worshiped. You were overcome by the majesty and glory and beauty. You *had* to say something. You *had* to exclaim. As Christians, that's what we do when we encounter God. He is holy and infinite and good and just and loving and on and on. We experience him, and we want to collapse on the ground, and we want to dance. We have to— we *have to*—say aloud, 'You are great! You are holy! You are above all else! I bow before you, and I worship you. You are God!'"

MacGregor paused again. "Do you see that?"

Lauren nodded again. She couldn't explain it, but she again felt that enchanting pull to what the professor was saying and at the same time a barely controllable urge to flee and hide. It was so beautiful and so strange and frightful, all at the same time. *What am I doing?* she wondered.

MacGregor said, "Gang, I need to go. Lauren, thank you for sharing with us about your god and for being honest about your reservations about Christianity. And thank you for allowing us to talk about the attributes of our God." He winked. "I really appreciate your letting me come. I love this kind of stuff. You've given me the gift of a good evening."

Jarrod responded enthusiastically, "Same here, Professor. I loved this too, but I feel like I never got around to some of the debates we've had in the past. I would love to do this again if you don't mind. I've never really learned that much about doctrine. I mean, I can tell you a fair amount about the philosophy of religion, and I can tell you a lot about worship and miracles, but we've never been much into doctrine at my church."

"I feel the same way," said Brad. "It's been stimulating. I did learn a lot of teachings growing up, but I think it was all pitched more at a youth-level understanding. Hearing you today makes me realize that I need to get an adult understanding of these teachings."

"Lauren?"

"I'm really enjoying this too. You bring a fresh perspective to our Sunday get-together, that's for sure. And"—she sighed and looked at each of them quickly—"while I don't like having my beliefs picked apart, you're making me rethink some things. But, honestly, I have to say I'm a bit scared of your God. I'm torn, but I think I might want to hear more."

Then she remembered something. "But you said you'd deal with the issue of Brad's intolerance. You know, the whole not dating people who aren't Christians."

MacGregor considered this for a moment. "You're right, I did say that, and I'm glad you reminded me. OK. Lauren, those extremist Christians you have mentioned back home in Baton Rouge and at UT, do you *really* want to date or marry one of those?"

"Heavens no," exclaimed Lauren.

"That's right. Think about it. There might be really good reasons for you not to marry one of those extremists. Marriage between somebody like you and somebody like that would be complicated and hard, don't you think? You already know this: marriage is hard under the best of circumstances.

"And remember what you said earlier, about being frustrated by these handsome guys who end up not being communicators? You said you wanted to know a guy intimately, and you wanted to be known. That assumes a level of security but also of shared core commitments. Do you really want to know one of those extremists intimately or have one of them know you intimately?"

"No."

"When you think of the guy you marry, don't you want him to be your soul mate? Someone you can commit to be with and he commits to you, and you share life—you do life together."

"Yes, that's exactly what I want."

"Well, if a Christian loves Jesus Christ more than any other person or thing, if living for Christ is the core of core commitments, wouldn't it stand to reason that that Christian is only going to find the best marriage with someone who loves God just as much? It's about both the man and the woman sharing the most important commitment— Christ—even before their commitment to each other. God is not some closed-minded ogre trying to stir up bigotry, but rather his command for Christians to unite their souls only with other Christians who place Christ above all else is for everyone's benefit. It's smart. It's practical. Does that make sense?"

Lauren pondered these words, looking vacantly across the coffeeshop. She sighed and looked at Brad for a moment and then back at MacGregor. "Yeah, I mean, it makes sense. But somehow I just can't lose the sense that there's something narrow and judgmental involved. But I do want to share the most important things with whomever I marry, and I guess I would always be looking to pick at a husband who was an extremist Christian. I don't know. My mind says one thing, but the whole thing still doesn't feel right. I still feel discriminated against."

"I understand," said MacGregor. "It's perfectly natural to feel that way. Whatever you do or believe, I hope you will find a guy who will love you and will share the most important things of life. I want you to be happy."

Distinct pleasantness pervaded the table. They grinned at one another because the resolution felt good after the earlier tension. Brad finally interrupted the quiet. "Professor, I think I'm speaking for all of us; will you join us in two weeks for our next Sunday evening time at Common Grounds? I think we all want to explore this a bit more."

"Brad, thank you. All of you, thanks. I am honored, and I will look forward to it. Is there anything in particular you want to talk about? Either from talking about God's character or one of the old issues you debate?"

The three friends looked at each other and shrugged. Jarrod said, "Nah, let's just go with the flow. Something's bound to come up. Let's just let the chips fall where they may."

Chapter 5

God's Schedule

PEOPLE ARE SO IN THE WAY, Brad thought as he deftly navigated the crowded sidewalk. How could so many people not have to work on Columbus Day? Just because the stock market wasn't open didn't mean the investment bankers didn't have to work. It only meant a slightly easier day and a rare chance to have lunch away from the office.

The holiday crowds filled all the parking places in this particular midtown nook, forcing him to walk a long way to meet Lauren, Jarrod, and Professor MacGregor for lunch at Common Grounds. Walking briskly, briefcase in tow, he kept his sights about twenty feet in front. He twisted one way, narrowly missing a slow-moving senior, cut left, left again, and then darted through another hole that momentarily opened up in the mass of pedestrians. It was like his pseudoglory days as an option quarterback for Coach MacMillan's veer offense, picking the holes and anticipating angles of pursuit. *These people are making me late,* he growled silently.

† † †

She could only occasionally leave the office for a coffee shop run, but a good day became a great day when Lauren could stop in at Common Grounds. She loved mixing it up with the diverse people who hung around this area, especially at her place. Lively, funny, interested in others, Lauren lit people up. She, in turn, was lit up by them, and these days there was something besides the caffeine that had her so enamored of her coffeehouse. In the wake of her frustration with Dr. Ffier and the episode with Brad, Lauren opened herself more to male attention. She enjoyed a good rapport with all the servers, but her favorite was Drex. Lauren didn't know what his real or full name was, but Drex was what he had said when he introduced himself to her. He was a little out there with his earring and tattoos, especially for professional Lauren. Though she wholeheartedly embraced her identity as a corporate attorney, suits and all, the decorum required of professionals could stultify the spirit. Clubbing and the bar scene provided Lauren with the typical outlet with coworkers and old friends from UT, but Drex as an individual presented a distinct and unusual remedy for her ego still smarting over the Brad episode. Drex appealed to all kinds of things inside her, and there was safety in knowing that nothing serious could ever come of anything with him. A fling with a bad boy, especially a really sweet bad boy, could be just what the doctor ordered.

She looked at him as he worked on her order. Drex exhibited an unusual kindness toward people. Gentle. This day he said he wanted to whip up a special confection for Lauren.

† † †

Brad knew that the Spinnaker deal he was working on was a bit of a long shot. He was trying to impress his boss, Julian Roth, but he found out his potential client was also being wooed by bankers from other firms. Julian apparently wasn't the only genius who thought up these propositions. Still, Richmond Steinberg could win the contract. The late nights and extra hours of number crunching would be worth it if he could land this client. But now he needed a shot of legal crack to kill the fatigue from weeks of sleep deficit. He couldn't believe he'd committed to lunch, even on Columbus Day.

A few more dodges and quick steps and Brad could see the coffee-house awning. He was already calculating how to grab the server's attention and call out his order in the most efficient way possible. Every second counted, and he wanted to snag his sandwich and coffee as soon as he could. He couldn't stop for long and even spend time with Professor MacGregor.

† † †

Perhaps this is proof that there is a God, Lauren smiled to herself as she sipped Drex's concoction. How else to explain the divine taste of the frozen mocha cappuccino? She checked her watch again. Brad was late, no surprise. Ditto with Jarrod. But she kind of expected the professor to be punctual; that was just the way of responsible adults. Lauren decided to wait at the tables outside and enjoy the cool temperatures of fall, or at least the Houston version of cool. She sipped again and waved to Drex as she backed out the door onto the sidewalk.

Drex motioned energetically, but he wasn't waving good-bye; he saw Brad's imminent arrival through the window. Lauren misunderstood his wave, and Drex watched helplessly as she stepped backward out the door, waving all the more merrily. Drex cringed. This was going to get ugly.

Boom! Brad in all his hurry ran smack into Lauren, who had just turned with her drink. The lid on the cup yielded to physics, and frozen mocha flew all over Brad's Brooks Brothers suit.

"What are you doing?" Brad yelled. "You've ruined my suit!" Then he recognized Lauren. Usually friendship and familiarity protect from angry outbursts; on some occasions, however, that same familiarity allows for more toxic venting than a stranger would receive. "Dang, Lauren!" Having his suit ruined before going back to work ticked him off. What was she thinking?

Lauren, mortified, reached to wipe some of the brown liquid off the jacket with a napkin that came with the cappuccino, but she seemed only to press it further into the fabric. "I'm so *so* sorry," she exclaimed. "Really, I didn't see you. I was just saying good-bye to my friend as I was heading out—"

"And you didn't *look* where you were going," Brad interrupted curtly. "Good grief, where did you learn how to walk?" Weeks of insecurely corked stress exploded, and Brad glowered at Lauren. How in the world could he make his postlunch meeting now?

Drex arrived with paper towels to sponge up the mess on the pavement and daub at Brad's suit as Lauren collected herself to speak.

"I really am sorry. But it's not like I did this to you intentionally, Brad. It was an *accident*. I'll pay to have your suit cleaned. I am sorry. But you don't need to get so mad at me, and you definitely need to lose that tone of voice with me." She felt bad about the suit, but Lauren was beginning to feel a lot less bad, thinking that Brad actually deserved it. Frankly, Brad's attitude surprised her. Where was her old friend, the All-American guy with the courtly charm? She had no idea he could be this much of a demanding jerk, and she had known him for years. That a close friend could act so out of character disturbed her.

"Maybe I can help."

Lauren eyed the new arrival with gratitude, for it was Professor MacGregor with a concerned countenance. Brad immediately looked caught and embarrassed when he realized that the professor probably witnessed some of his invective toward Lauren.

Before he did anything else, MacGregor gave Lauren a hug and said, "Sorry that this happened. It's going to work out just fine, I think. And it's good to see you. For a casual workday you are dressed sensationally." He beamed at her.

"Thank you. And it's really good to see you too. I was excited about lunch with you, but now I'm *really* glad to see you. But how do you think this is going to work out? I really have ruined his jacket."

"We'll see." Turning to Brad, he extended his hand and said, "Brad, good to see you." Brad shook his hand and felt the warmth in the older man's eyes. "Tough break with the spill," he continued. "As I walked up, I heard you say you were going to miss a meeting. I understand your being upset. Let's see if there's a way to remedy this situation."

"OK. What do you suggest?" asked Brad with detectable doubt.

"I know the owner of the cleaners a few doors down. I bet I can get him to fix your suit jacket up lickety-split."

Brad's face evinced a mix of skepticism and hope. "Are you sure? Won't that take awhile?"

"Well, you were going to grab a sandwich with us anyway, weren't you? This may take a little longer but not much."

The professor's sense of confidence and kindness sapped some of Brad's ill will. "Thank you." But there was still the issue of his all-important meeting. More softly than before he said, "I have a meeting in less than an hour. There's *no way* anyone can clean my suit fast enough to make it on time. I left myself just enough time to grab a bite to eat with you all and scoot. I'll never make it now."

"You're right. You won't make it now. But the whole afternoon doesn't have to be shot. Let me take your suit jacket to the cleaners, and let's see how quickly we can get you fixed up. Either way, you need to get your jacket cleaned, right?" MacGregor smiled that bemused smile of his.

"Good point. I'll take your offer, and I'll call the VP and see if I can postpone our meeting a little bit." Brad began to transfer the contents of his jacket pockets to his pants pockets and briefcase, and no sooner had he slipped the jacket off and given it to MacGregor than his cell phone rang.

"This is Brad. Yes. Yes. OK, well that works out great for me too. All right. I'll see him at 3:00. Great. Bye." Brad looked up, astonished but grinning. "That was the vice president's assistant. He's had something come up and had to postpone until 3:00. I'm not going to miss my meeting after all. Go figure."

"Go figure," said MacGregor, the smile still on his face. "I'm going to run your jacket to my friend at the cleaners, and then I'll be right back."

As MacGregor walked down the street, Lauren felt relieved and said, "I'm so glad this is working out." Then she remembered what a startling performance Brad gave in his pedestrian rage, and she felt the whole thing was an accident for which both could stand to apologize. She added puckishly, "But you know, you *did* spill my drink. I think you owe me a new cup of coffee." She winked.

She accomplished her goal. Brad's eyes narrowed just a bit in mock militant posture. "Whatever. But don't worry about the suit. Mistakes happen." Having run the gamut from irritation and impatience to shock and anger to embarrassment and on to relief, all in a space of four minutes, Brad felt off balance, but his natural instinct for humor was the right one. This was a game he knew. "And I'll buy you lunch, not because I owe you but just to be gallant." It was Brad's turn to wink.

Drex busied himself with the new orders, relieved that Brad and Lauren restored peace; and by the time he finished, MacGregor returned to order something for himself. MacGregor looked at Brad and Lauren and asked, "Where's Jarrod? Should we wait to order sandwiches or go ahead?"

"I'll call him," said Brad. He felt the need to perform good deeds to get back in the good graces of this Christian figure he respected so greatly. He thought to himself that calling Jarrod might not exactly serve as a substitute for penance or making a pilgrimage to the Holy Land, but instinctively he had to do something good.

Just as Brad started to punch the digits on his phone, Jarrod strolled in, pushing his now lengthy blonde locks out of his eyes.

"Hey, guys. Sorry I'm late. Parking was a bear. So what's up?"

The silence, followed by reluctant grins, which finally gave way to laughter, told him something had happened. Brad told Jarrod his highly selective version, focusing on Lauren's proclivity for backward ambulation through doorways, which elicited more chuckles. Lauren thought of responding but then realized that even if she spun the story, it would make Brad look bad for real. She decided to let Brad's version be the official one because it was so clearly over-the-top.

MacGregor shook Jarrod's hand and thanked him for coming.

"Absolutely. I wouldn't miss it." Jarrod now noticed MacGregor's attire. "Nifty tweed," he said approvingly.

"It's fall," MacGregor replied simply. "Nice sandals."

"You like these? I won 'em off a buddy who didn't think I could still get up on a surfboard. But I'd pay cash money for that bow tie you're wearing."

"You like it? I won it off a buddy who didn't think I could still dunk." That broke them all up as they migrated over to their table in the corner, waiting for Drex to bring their lunch. Once seated, MacGregor tossed out a little conversational bomb.

"I love a day that proceeds right on schedule."

No one knew how to react to that. Finally Brad asked, "What do you mean? What kind of schedule are you on?"

MacGregor looked at each one of them, his eyes twinkling, obviously testing them. "Well, of course, I'm on God's schedule. And the good news is, so are you."

Jarrod looked at MacGregor and then at Lauren and Brad. "What do you mean, we're on God's schedule?" asked Jarrod, intrigued.

Brad jumped first. "If you'll remember, Spirit's Power, Jarrod's church, emphasizes God's power being *all over* the place.

"Sounds promiscuous," said the professor with a twinkle in his eye. The others smiled but really had no idea what he meant.

Brad continued, "And yet the ideas of order, schedule, and structure are foreign to them." *Ding*, the next sparring match had begun.

"Or, more charitably," Lauren said, "Jarrod takes this question seriously. You remember he's at Rice, doing his graduate work in philosophy. What Brad is leaving out is this class back in college. Jarrod agonized over the whole determinism/free will debate and had us all talking about it. But that was one religious topic, maybe the only one, where we all agreed."

"Thanks, guys. I guess one of the benefits of having old friends is that they can talk for you." Jarrod chuckled. "But they're right, even Brad my oppressor. My church definitely does not talk about 'God and schedules.' Come to think of it, I've never heard language like this from any Christian that I personally know. What did you mean, God has a schedule?"

"I mean God has a schedule that includes all of us. It's a good schedule. We don't always like the way a day unfolds. Some folks dislike the entire *life* that unfolds for them. But that doesn't mean that it's not a schedule and a good one."

Brad felt irritated again. What was all this schedule talk about God? And what about all the bad things that happen? His Baptist roots ran deep, and the thing he was surest of in all the world was that he had free will. "What are you saying? That we're all in some celestial Day-Timer? That God's got us entered into his Palm Pilot?"

"I suppose you could say he has us in his hands." An amused expression crept back across MacGregor's face. "Why? Is what I'm saying to you *really* so foreign? Don't you *believe* in God?"

In stereo Brad and Jarrod quickly answered, "Yes," and Brad continued, "Of *course,* I believe in God."

Lauren, though, looked surprised and twisted uncomfortably in her chair. "Why do you ask?" Obviously the professor knew they each believed in God because they detailed their respective beliefs about God last time. *What is he getting at?* she wondered.

"It's an important question," replied MacGregor, "perhaps the *most* personal question and a very important one. But I would say that there is an equally important question."

MacGregor again let it hang in the air, and his words reverberated several times through the minds of Jarrod, Lauren, and Brad. Brad thought, *OK, we're playing a game here. Fine. I'll ask.*

"OK, what would that equally important question be?"

"'What god?' of course."

Jarrod jumped in, "Exactly. You're asking *what* God we believe in." To Brad he said, "He's saying that not only is it important to ask, '*Do* you believe in God?' but it's also important to ask, '*What* is that God like?' Remember last time how different our understandings of God were?"

"Right," Lauren agreed.

Lauren's eyes met the older gentleman's, searching for a clue to understand what he was getting at. The topic made her nervous. She had definite ideas about religious fanatics, and talking about religion in public with someone she barely knew definitely qualified as awkward.

MacGregor's eyes met Lauren's searching gaze, and again she sensed him to be warm and kind and *knowing*. He seemed to be able to see right into her. The realization startled her, and she averted her eyes for a moment before asking a question.

"What do you do again? Brad just mentioned something about the seminary."

"I teach Christian theology. I've taught at the seminary here, but I retired two years ago. I still teach one class a semester, but I'm officially retired."

He continued. "I asked the question, 'Do you believe in God, and really, what god do you believe in?' because God is a part of all that I do. Our days do happen on schedule—God's schedule—and it's a good one. This awareness permeates my days. I've believed this so long and embraced it—*leaned* upon it—for so long that I don't see how I can be me and *not* talk about the Lord's undergirding every moment throughout my day. Does that make sense?"

The guys all took Lauren's bewildered stare to mean no. She didn't say anything, but it was apparent that the professor might as well have spoken Swahili. Whatever he had just said arrived untranslated to her ears.

Brad looked at the older man. *This* was interesting. He remembered both Jarrod's accusation of his darkened heart and his realization at the same time that he had let most aspects of his faith in Christ slide. MacGregor's words reminded him that he wished he were more clued in about his faith.

"That's incredible. Just recently I've decided that I need to get back in step with God. And here we are, you talking about God's being part of your whole day. That's exactly what I need. Go figure."

"Go figure?" MacGregor asked. "You think our getting together was an accident?"

"No, not an accident. But you have to admit this is a coincidence that I saw you speak, invited you to join our conversations, and something I realize I need is something that's important to you."

"What do you mean by *coincidence?*"

"You know, when things come together by chance."

"How is that different from an accident?"

Brad didn't answer. How *was* chance different from accident? It wasn't. The professor had him.

MacGregor picked up the conversation again. "Your hearing me speak is no coincidence. The three of us being Christians is no coincidence. The three of you having this wonderful friendship for years is no coincidence. Lauren spilling her drink on your suit, your boss calling to postpone your meeting—these are not coincidences. As I said before, it's all happening on schedule—God's schedule. And isn't it wonderful?"

MacGregor was in his element, winsomely speaking truth. *How can he make something so strange seem even remotely attractive?* Lauren wondered in spite of herself. "Look, I believe in God, as I said last time. I'm into spirituality, just not into organized religion. I don't understand why you say God has a schedule. I've never heard that before." She found the unpleasantness subsiding and felt a growing fascination with the professor.

"Lauren, you raise an excellent question. What I really mean is that God is in control of the universe. He really is Lord. He rules. And this ruling of the universe, including our lives, flows out of his character. He doesn't rule like a cruel despot; rather, he rules with grace, truth, love, mercy, and justice. God governs all our lives this way because that's who he is."

Jarrod nodded. "When you put it that way, it makes more sense. I do believe that God is the ruler of all. But still, what you're saying sounds as if he planned for Lauren to spill her mocha drink on Brad, which makes it sound as if God planned to waste the special drink Drex whipped up for her," he concluded with a sly grin. Lauren ignored him.

MacGregor replied, "Well, that is a good point. As you might suspect, this is a question Christian theologians have wrestled with for centuries. There are two parts to this issue. The first is whether God plans in advance for things to happen. The second is God's current governing of the universe."

Lauren asked, "Do you believe that God plans things in advance? Like Jarrod said, do you believe God planned for me to spill that drink?"

"Lauren, this is a complicated question you ask. The short answer is, 'Yes, I do believe that God plans things in advance. I believe that your run-in with Mr. Masterson was not a surprise to God.'"

This was too much for Brad. "How can you say that? You make it sound as if everything that happens, good or bad, is up to God. That's crazy! You know I believe in God, and I'm strongly committed to him. But in terms of the events of my daily life, I do my own thing. I know Christ is my personal Lord and Savior, but *I* live my life."

MacGregor gazed at him kindly for a moment. "Brad, I would never say you are an inadequate Christian. And I am impressed that you are faithful in worship and service. Of course you live your own life—who else can live it for you?" He paused. "But I guess you don't pray."

Brad was not the only one shocked by this. Jarrod and Lauren were also a bit taken aback. While the professor said these words in the same gentle way he said everything else, the content of his words was piercing.

"What do you mean, I don't pray?"

"Well, do you?"

"Of course I pray. Everybody prays. I mean, I don't pray *all* the time. And the past couple of months, I haven't prayed as much as I'd like." Brad, for the first time, was on his heels. A crack appeared in his professional veneer, and he looked vulnerable on this matter. However, the professor wouldn't let his new friend twist in the wind.

"Brad, I'm not actually asking about your personal devotional habits. Besides, the Father loves you *completely* anyway, whether you pray lots or little. What I meant by saying, 'I guess you don't pray,' is that given your statement about living your *own* life and that it's crazy to think that God governs the universe, it would seem that there's no point in praying. If you are the captain of your soul and the master of your fate, why pray?"

Jarrod jumped in, "Brad prays. We've prayed for things together over the years. After all, we're supposed to pray. I mean, for *lots* of things. Help with school, fighting spiritual darkness, for sick people. But that doesn't mean we aren't in control of our lives. At my church they teach us to pray for all that stuff, and yet we're very much in control."

"Exactly," said Lauren. "I believe in God, and I pray when I am feeling spiritual. Of course, I'm not a Christian and haven't gone to Mass since I was a child, but I do pray occasionally. And I'm still in control of *my* life."

"What I hear you guys saying is that you know God, you believe in God, but he doesn't govern your lives. Is that right?"

Lauren, Brad, and Jarrod looked at one another and back at MacGregor. "Sort of," said Jarrod. "I mean, I believe God is God, but I still make my own decisions."

"I agree with that. We all make our own decisions, our own choices. But here's the question: Does God have control over your lives, and does he have control over the world?"

All three squirmed uncomfortably. This was exciting but agonizing at the same time. What was the professor getting at anyway?

MacGregor spoke again. "Here's the deal: if God is not in control of our lives, others' lives, and the world, why pray? What good does it do to make requests when God lacks the ability, *the capacity,* to do anything about it? If God can't do anything in my life or your life or others' lives, then praying is only a therapeutic exercise. We're saying, 'Talking to God is cheaper than paying for a counselor or therapist. I get things off my chest to God, but all he can do is sit and listen because he can't do anything about it.' Why? He doesn't have control, he doesn't govern, he doesn't rule."

Lauren blinked and mused privately that prayer sounded more useful and certainly more economical than sessions with Dr. Ffeir.

Long pauses were becoming a regular feature of conversation with MacGregor. They pondered the professor's words for a moment, and then Jarrod replied. "I don't get what you're saying. My whole Christian life I've been taught to pray, and I've read those passages in the Bible where Jesus is praying. I like praying. But I keep feeling that you're saying God has to be in *control* of me, and that's just bogus."

MacGregor said, "Jarrod, I know. Believe me, I *know.* Let me try coming at this another way. Do you have any friends who are not believers?"

"Yeah, I've got a couple of friends who aren't believers. Actually, most of my friends probably don't believe. But there are a couple of them that I talk to about God. I talk to them about Christ and his love sometimes."

"Jarrod, that's terrific. The fact that you're still friends with them shows them that you love them, that you care about them as people regardless of what they believe. It sounds as if you are being Jesus to them."

At the professor's warm words Jarrod grinned in spite of himself. Again he felt drawn to this older man.

"But what I want to know is this: Do you pray for them? Do you pray that they will come to faith in Christ?"

"Of *course* I do," said Jarrod. "All the time."

"Who are you praying to that your friends will come to believe?"

"Well, God, of course. Who else would I be praying to?"

"What are you asking God to do?" MacGregor asked this question deliberately, speaking each word slowly.

"To make them Christians."

"To do what?"

"To make them Christians. To change their hearts."

"But if *they* are in control of their lives, and God is *not* in control of their lives, how could he possibly answer your prayer? Besides, are you aware of what you're saying? Listen to your own words: *make* them Christians, *change* their hearts. You're asking God to do things to them and make them something they are not. If God answered your prayers, wouldn't he be controlling them to some degree?"

Jarrod was quiet. That made a lot of sense. Why *was* he praying for Todd and Brandon if God couldn't do anything to them? Of course God could do stuff in their lives. He knew that. After all, God had changed his own life. And if God could work in Todd and Brandon's lives and if he had already changed his own life, God must be in control. It made sense, but why was he feeling so uptight about this "God in control" stuff? Really, *why?*

Brad put it all together. "So you're saying that if people pray, then they are asking God to do things in peoples' lives. And if God is doing things in their lives, then they don't have control. OK. I can see your thinking about prayer and God having power, but you are still taking it too far when you say God has a schedule. He can 'schedule' his own activities, but maybe he can't schedule other peoples' lives. In other words, he knows how he can intervene personally and cause things to happen in a life, but that doesn't mean everything is under God's control."

Brad felt good. This was good. He would concede on the prayer thing; he was on weak ground to argue the opposite. But he had come up with a viable alternative that protected what he knew to be true, that he was still in control of his life *most* of the time.

MacGregor looked at Brad for a moment. It was that searching look of his but always accompanied with kindly eyes. "Brad, how about we examine what Scripture says? Would that be all right?"

"Sure. But it sounds like I am about to get whacked or 'lose my religion.' So before this gets any deeper, I could sure use a refill on my drink and something to add to the sandwich. That just wasn't enough food, no matter how cute Lauren thinks Drex is." She rolled her eyes but otherwise didn't respond. "Anyone else for a warm-up?"

"Good idea. I'll top off everyone's drinks," offered Jarrod. He collected everyone's cup and followed Brad to the counter as the others stretched their legs. He was curious about where this conversation was heading.

Chapter 6

9/11 and God's Schedule

AFTER THEY HAD DALLIED getting their respective coffees to optimal tastes with creams and sugars, they all repaired to their table in the corner. MacGregor reached into his tweed jacket and pulled out his worn, slender Bible.

"The questions on the table have to do with God's sovereignty with respect to humans and the world, how much control or freedom there is, and whether we can legitimately speak of events as happening on schedule. Agreed?"

They each signaled their agreement, and MacGregor began.

"I'm going to turn to Paul's letter to the Ephesians, chapter 1." He pulled out some reading glasses, and his fingers slipped through the tissue-soft pages until he came to Ephesians 1. Turning the Bible around so Brad could see it, the professor invited Brad to read verse 11.

"Just verse 11 or read past that?" asked Brad.

"Oh, verse 11 and verse 12, I believe."

Brad looked down and read: "In him we were also chosen, having been predestined according to the plan of him who works out everything in conformity with the purpose of his will, in order that we, who were the first to hope in Christ, might be for the praise of his glory."

Brad looked up and said, "Is this about predestination? I really, *really* don't like that whole debate. It just seems like *such* a waste of time to me." He was getting irritated again.

"No, don't worry. I don't want to get into the predestination issue today either. Yes, verse 11 mentions the word, and in the context of chapter 1 the apostle Paul is definitely writing about the subject of predestination. But what I want to direct your attention to is what follows the word 'predestined' in verses 11 and 12. Brad, if you would please, read what comes after 'predestined.'"

Brad read again, "According to the plan of him who works out everything in conformity with the purpose of his will."

MacGregor continued, "According to the what?"

"The purpose," Lauren answered.

"Yes, the purpose. And it's the purpose of God. And what does God work out?"

There was another long silence. Brad, Lauren, and Jarrod took turns looking at the open Bible before them on the table. They could each hear the words they read repeating over and over in their minds. MacGregor gently asked again, "What does God work out?"

"Everything," said Jarrod with resignation. He slumped in his chair and sighed. All three looked as if they had received coal in their Christmas stockings.

"You look morose!" said MacGregor. "Why the long faces?"

"Because," Brad said dejectedly, "I pride myself on knowing the Bible pretty well, and I would have bet a thousand dollars that nothing like this was in the Bible. I've never heard this in my life, and I've been in church since I was born.

"Another reason is that it goes against most things I've ever heard in church. This verse, at least on the face of it, means what I've heard is wrong. And it's not just some Bible trivia I'm wrong about. This is pretty core; it means I'm wrong about something that I've *known* was absolutely true."

"What do you mean?" asked Lauren, who appeared angry and was looking to draw statements out of Brad to marshal against MacGregor's new and appalling proposition.

"Well, like you, one of the key principles of my life is the fact that *I'm in control.* I make my own way. I work hard, think smart, and success follows. You are the same. This is exactly how you live your life and what you believe.

"Professor," Brad continued, "you're telling me that something I've built my *whole* life on is wrong. That's a bit overwhelming, you know?"

Jarrod nodded his agreement.

Lauren, feeling threatened, couldn't contain her anger any longer. Facing MacGregor across the table, she let loose. "Yeah, it definitely freaks me out. What are you saying, that I'm a *puppet?*" She bit the last word off in anger. "That we're all puppets? That we live this *illusion* that we're making choices, but in reality we're just dolls on a string for God. So is God just some cosmic puppeteer? Is my life, is the whole world, just some kind of sick joke?"

"No, no, no. Lauren, I'm not saying that at all. Your life is precious and significant. Your choices and decisions in this world are real and significant. You are most definitely not a puppet on a string."

MacGregor paused.

"And besides, it's not me who's saying it. Look at who you're getting mad at—who is the author of Scripture?"

It was a rhetorical question and a potent one. Even though Lauren didn't personally believe the Bible, the culture in which she had grown up had enough Judeo-Christian residue that she knew many people considered it the Word of God. She understood this and thus respected the Bible in some sense, even though she didn't actually believe it.

"Lauren, please. I meant what I said; your life *is* wonderful and significant. You are not a puppet on a string. But God is in charge of the whole shootin' match, and that should give us comfort."

"How can you say we're *not* puppets?! It's so plain right there in that verse! The word is 'everything' right? He plans ev-er-y-thing!" Lauren pronounced each syllable belligerently.

Brad felt torn, as though watching a tennis match. After the professor spoke, he reluctantly felt MacGregor had a point—the verse in God's Word *did* say God had a plan for everything. But when Lauren responded with such grit, he secretly cheered, since she was carrying his flag.

Something suddenly clicked in Brad's mind. Emboldened by Lauren's passion, he put his new question to MacGregor. "Professor, if what you're saying is true, how does this relate to 9/11? I mean, according to what you're saying, God basically flew the planes into the World Trade Center and the Pentagon. I'm sorry, but I just can't sign off on that. Too many innocent people died. I don't buy it."

Jarrod looked at the professor. "Yeah. What about September 11?"

MacGregor started to answer, then checked himself. He looked down at his hands for what seemed like a long time before his eyes rose to meet each of their gazes for a moment. He sighed. "You don't know what you're asking. That is a huge topic, with so much emotion involved. I can't answer you. I can respond to your question, I can send words in your direction, but how does anybody answer the 9/11 question?"

He shook his head. "At the anniversary, I thought I was OK. But then, it hit me all over again as I saw interviews with children and spouses of the firemen, the policemen, and the employees in the towers. To answer you means I would be able to answer them, and I can't.

"It's not a matter of where do I pick up the theological pieces when the grieving is done. As I learned last month for the hundredth time in my life, grieving is never done. This may seem strange to you young people, and I don't want to inject awkwardness into our new friendship, but for weeks after 9/11 I wept. Hearing a spouse express hope that the husband or wife would be rescued, hearing children ask why daddy wasn't home, I just wept.

"Even if the grieving *were* over at some point, if I could be all cleaned up, it's not like *that's* when I put my theological puzzle back together. My theology—I should say, my knowing the Lord—was critical before 9/11, on 9/11, and every day after. I had no answers then, and I have no answers now. What I did have on that awful day, and what I continue to have, is hope."

Testily, Lauren asked, "How can you have hope? It was the most terrible thing I've ever experienced. Anger, I understand. Or depression. But *hope?* I don't get how anyone could have hope."

"Because the final word on those people in the planes, the people in the Pentagon and in New York, the final word is not death. The suffering has been real and unending for all those people. I mean, I see it on their faces. The pain is intense, and for many it's still raw. But as real and long and deep as that suffering is, it's not the final word.

"We marvel that Osama bin Laden could send underlings to murder themselves and others like this. And if I may take a quick tangent, they were murderers, not martyrs. The word *martyr* is a Greek word meaning 'a witness.' In the Christian tradition the church applied the word *martyr* to believers who were persecuted because they witnessed for Christ by refusing to recant their faith. They were jailed, beaten, tortured, and often slaughtered. They endured the torture and the killing by their persecutors, and thus they gave powerful testimony, or witness, for Christ. There is no parallel to what these young terrorists did, who took it upon themselves to murder thousands. I am called to love and forgive them, and I've often asked the Lord to give me grace to love them and forgive them. But I don't want any confusion, any falsity about the term *martyr* and its being applied to terrorists."

Lauren didn't respond, but Brad and Jarrod murmured quiet agreement.

"But back to what I was saying. Why do I have hope? I have hope because my heavenly Father also lost someone. While it is a marvel that bin Laden would send young men to slaughter others as they did on

9/11, what is more marvelous is that the Father would send his Son to die for us.

"Believe me, being an older man and a theologian doesn't make me less human. I felt rage toward those hijackers and those who support them. But that day and in the aftermath, as fury and rage and grief and lack of comprehension and love for the firemen and the policemen and my faltering attempts to forgive the terrorists all swirled around, I kept running into one thing that gave me hope—the cross.

"The cross doesn't trivialize the pain. It doesn't make it go away. But I have hope because God understands what it is to suffer, to hurt, to grieve, to long for."

"But if you're right, God could have stopped the planes!" Brad exclaimed.

"Really? If you are asking whether the Lord possesses the power to stop planes, or awaken an airport security guard's mind so that he apprehends the hijackers before they get on the plane, or awaken the INS so they don't let them in the country, or on and on, yes, the Lord possesses the power to stop that."

"Then why didn't he?" Lauren shot back. "It makes no sense! If he has the power, how can he let this go on?"

Again MacGregor sighed. Again he paused, looking down. "I don't know, Lauren. I don't know. It's not a matter of impotence. Rabbi Kushner came to that conclusion in his famous book *When Bad Things Happen to Good People.* He believes God lacks the ability to do anything to alleviate suffering, but that is not what Scripture or the church says.

"All things are under his control. Still, peoples' wicked desires, their murderous acts—these they do will on their own. Their human wills operate within God's control. Every sin, every wicked act is the responsibility of that person or persons. God is not responsible for the evil. Blame does not besmirch God's holy character. But here's the mystery. God ordains it all, the good and the bad, and mysteriously enfolds peoples' good and evil desires into his overall plan."

"That's what the verse means about everything working according to his plan?" asked Lauren.

MacGregor agreed, "Yes, that's right, Lauren. The Scripture says God works out everything. And how does he carry out this work? According to the purpose of his will. *His will.* I know you said you're not a Christian, but do you know the story of Jesus' being betrayed and crucified?"

Lauren nodded, and MacGregor continued, "You may not remember this, but the night he was betrayed, Jesus had a last supper with his disciples." Jarrod and Brad nodded, as did Lauren. She had only a vague understanding of what it meant, but in her early childhood she and her family had gone to Mass every week. The memory was bittersweet— sweet at the recollection of the whole family together and happy, but bitter because it eventually all fell to pieces.

"After dinner Jesus took his closest disciples and went to a place called the Garden of Gethsemane. He asked his closest disciples to pray, and then he walked a short distance away." Turning to Brad and Jarrod, he said, "Remember how anxious he was and what he did? He *prayed.* What did he pray? 'Father, if you are willing, take this cup from me. Yet not my will but Yours be done.' Jesus *knew* his Father, and Jesus *trusted* the will of his Father. Imagine facing something as awful as torture and crucifixion and saying, 'I trust your will, Father.' How can Jesus trust his Father's will? Because he knows the Father and he knows the Father's will is good."

Jarrod interrupted, "Yeah, but he's Jesus, not us. He's different. You can't say that the same thing applies to us."

"Do you think the will of the Father was better for Jesus? Jarrod, think about what you're saying. Jesus faced the cross. If Jesus knew the ultimate excruciating death that faced him and yet he could still trust the Father's will to be a good will, how can we think any less of his will in our circumstances? What are you going to be facing that's worse than bearing all of the sin of the world on the cross?"

It was Brad's turn to weigh in again. "OK, that's an excellent point. But how are we *not* puppets? On one hand we have this verse that says God works out everything. On the other hand you say that we make real and significant choices. How can you have it both ways? If God works out everything, how can I have a real choice?"

"Brad, you have put the question beautifully. Yes, this is the crux of the matter. How can God govern all things, and how can we have real and significant choices? The Bible teaches us both. And I love the answer to your question, which I mentioned a few minutes ago in conjunction with 9/11—it's a mystery! I *love* that. The Bible's teachings about God being in control and about us making real choices cannot be slotted, organized, figured out, and systematized. These two themes that the Bible teaches culminate in mystery. We, in our modernist tendencies, want to figure it all out precisely, to be clean and neat, to reconcile these conceptual enemies. However, as the English Baptist preacher Charles Spurgeon famously said when asked this question, 'I do not try to reconcile friends.' These matters are mystery to us, but they are not mysterious to God.

"I believe that God is sovereign over all things, and I believe that he allows us to make real choices. How these work together is a mystery. One of the great theologians in recent church history, Herman Bavinck, writes that when it comes to our doctrines, 'mystery is the crucial element.' I *love* the fact that it's a mystery because it seems to fit God so well. He *is* mysterious. God is awe inspiring. He is infinitely bigger than we are, and our puny minds simply can't figure out all this stuff. That's great."

MacGregor paused to give his new friends a chance to respond, but they were focused in rapt attention. He went on. "And do you know what mystery causes me to do? Mystery draws me in. The Lord calls me even more in his mysteriousness to seek him. And as I seek, I come to know him better, and the God that I'm coming to know is a good God, full of grace and truth, worthy of my worship."

Brad and Jarrod were on the edges of their seats. Even Lauren's animosity leaked out considerably, and she got caught up in the beauty of what MacGregor unspooled. *This* was getting interesting. There was something magnetic about the professor as he went deeper into his thoughts.

"So there's no really precise answer to my question?" asked Brad.

"No, there's not. We can walk only so far down the road of asking questions, and then we should go no further. I can only affirm what the Scriptures say, and the Scriptures reveal that God is sovereign over the world and that humans make real decisions. To go any further than the Scriptures is vain speculation."

"In spite of myself, I like it. I really do. I feel a ring of truth as you talk this out. But," Brad smiled, "this would never fly in the business world. People without answers find themselves on the outside looking in."

"But it *is* an answer," MacGregor replied. "It really is. The answer is mystery. In the marketplace, answers may need to be sharp, defined, calculable, and precise, but do you really want God to be that way? Would you really feel drawn to a God who is reducible to calculation and precision?"

Brad thought about this. Everything in his life was about precision, calculation, and numbers. Ambiguity was a bad thing. Being confident, or "highly confident" was a requisite buzzword in his world. He was so used to things being that way and so impatient when life at large didn't fall into place this way.

"But God has always seemed precise to me. That's how I've been raised. That's what I've been taught. Four steps to joy with God, five points on how to be Spirit filled, the ten principles of Christian growth. The God I've always heard about is a God you can know if you simply have the discipline to do the steps."

"And how awesome is that God to you?"

"He's very awesome."

"Really?" MacGregor asked with a lilt in his voice, taking the edge off a rather confrontational question.

"Yeah. Really," replied Brad evenly.

"How much time do you spend with God in the Bible and in prayer?"

Brad didn't answer.

"How much do you *long* to worship the Lord on the Lord's Day?"

Again Brad didn't answer.

"Brad, I ask these not to judge you or to check up on you or see how well you're performing. I used to have legalistic standards of how long and how often a devotional life was supposed to be in order for a person to be a 'good' Christian, but I dropped that years ago. I only ask these as diagnostic questions because my hunch is that if the God you've been reared to believe in is all precision and formulae, I can't imagine for a second that your heart is enticed to love or spend time with him."

Brad tried to control his countenance, but he was shocked at these questions and MacGregor's last statement. But the professor wasn't finished.

"How much do you find yourself yearning to do things that will make *God* look good?"

Again, no answer. MacGregor let this pause go for some time. And then, softly, "Do you miss him?"

Another mystery is how mere words can penetrate a human heart. In countless other challenging scenarios, this investment banker was impervious. Emotion did not have control over him. Yet, as Brad's spiritual life progressively dried up, and as he had recently realized it but done nothing about it, he was vulnerable to the kind professor's probe. Unquestionably, Brad missed God, and he missed him deeply. Brad felt a slight swell of emotion rising up, and he could feel his face also slightly reddening against his best efforts to control. The professional veneer, cracked earlier, now disappeared. Brad felt suddenly exposed. He didn't want to make eye contact, and he didn't want to answer. Not being in control in a social situation when his whole life was in control incited its own peculiar twinge of terror. Touching on this subject was way too close to home. He feared that if he spoke a tide of emotion might roll in.

"How long have you gone on this way? Weeks?" Brad nodded. "Months?" Brad nodded again.

The wise old professor asked again, "So you miss him?" This time Brad responded with a quick, barely perceptible nod. Unable to hide his exposure, Brad expected judgment. However, the grace in the professor's voice brought Brad's eyes up, and he looked at him. Only warmth and acceptance were coming back at him in MacGregor's gaze.

"Brad, you have tasted the Lord. You can't miss God unless you've tasted and seen that he is good. But while you tasted, you have been fed a God who is too small. A God too small doesn't attract your attention, doesn't entice your affection, doesn't demand your worship. A God of formulae and how-to steps doesn't command allegiance. Other things in the world have crowded the divine out of your life because your too-small God is not as awe inspiring as those things. People chase what they love, and the God you've been handed is not a God worth loving. At least not worth loving more than the things you chase instead."

Brad seemed incapable of doing anything but nodding. Jarrod and Lauren looked on, transfixed.

"The God of the Bible—the God of Abraham, Isaac, and Jacob—is a *huge* God. He is awe inspiring. He is powerful. He knows all. He is utterly holy. He never does wrong. He is truth and love. He is far above all other gods and far above us. His ways and thoughts are higher than ours. He is too big for us ever to know completely. What we can know of God we know because he lets us glimpse him in Jesus Christ, in his Word, and in creation. But this huge, incomprehensibly great God remains a mystery. He will always be a mystery."

More nodding from Brad.

"And you know why you don't pray much?"

Brad finally looked up. "No," he said softly.

"Because you believe it doesn't really matter. Deep down you really don't believe prayer works because with the stress you're under, you would do *anything* to succeed. Right?"

"Yes. I grab hold of anything that helps me accomplish my goals."

"And the reason you don't pray is because you don't believe prayer helps you accomplish your goals. If prayer worked, you'd do it. Since prayer doesn't work, why waste your time? And the reason prayer doesn't work, deep down, is because your God is too small. He can't respond to your prayers because he's not in control. Instead, *you're* in control, and you walk around with the weight of the world on your shoulders since it's all up to you."

"But I don't really think like that. You're making it seem as if I don't believe in prayer or God at all."

"Brad, think about it. By your own admission you don't pray much. Look, I know you believe in God and prayer in some sense. Of course you do. But because 'you're in control' and because your too-small God doesn't control things, it's useless to pray. In fact, since you're in control of your own life, the only one you should pray to is yourself."

The sting of that shocking phrase lingered pungently. For a kind old man, MacGregor could sure highlight some unkind realities.

The interaction between MacGregor and Brad mesmerized Lauren. Seeing Brad's vulnerability and the professor's challenging but gracious demeanor soothed her anxiety about this weird brand of religion. She found herself curious again.

"So you're saying that the reason we don't pray more is because we think God can't do anything? This just seems so strange to me, and I think it's strange to Brad and Jarrod too. Do you have anything else to support this? Why should we believe something that contradicts everything we've ever known simply because you read one verse?"

Jarrod agreed. "I mean, it's not like your Ephesians verse doesn't count, but is there anything else in the Bible that says this?"

"I'm glad you're skeptical," MacGregor replied. "I'm glad that someone like me can't just throw one Scripture at you and persuade you against everything you've ever heard. You're asking the right thing— show me from God's Word a little more that supports this view. So I will. Jarrod, would you please turn to Isaiah 46:9–10?"

Jarrod took the old Bible in his hands and began to flip through it ackwardly. Neither his enthusiasm for Jesus nor his enthusiasm for intellectual pursuits in philosophy had translated into reading the Bible much at all. MacGregor saw the aimless flipping and said, "You know how Psalms is kind of in the middle of the whole Bible? Open up to Psalms and then start turning right. Isaiah is a few books past Psalms."

Jarrod took the tips in stride and soon found the verse. "Read it out loud?" he asked.

"Please," MacGregor replied.

"OK. Isaiah 46, verses 9–10. 'Remember the former things, those of long ago; I am God, and there is no other; I am God, and there is none like me. I make known the end from the beginning, from ancient times, what is still to come. I say: My purpose will stand, and I will do all that I please.'"

Again Jarrod slumped back in his chair. "Wow!" he exclaimed. "I never knew that was in there. I've been a Christian since high school, and I've never heard anything like this."

MacGregor said, "And what is the context? The Lord is telling the people, whom he calls the 'house of Jacob' in verse 3, about himself. The Lord is asking his people to compare him to the idols of Babylon, which were crafted from gold and silver. He is telling them that this is the kind of God he is. How do you think they felt when they heard this?"

"I bet they felt pretty awesome. Here is their God saying, 'Yes, I am the *only* God, and I do what I want to do.' If he's their God and he's like this, then they are going to be a lot better off than the dudes with the gold idols." Jarrod was on a roll.

"Exactly, Jarrod. When God reveals to his people that he is the only God and that his purposes will stand, they can have confidence that things are going to work out."

Brad spoke up again, "This reminds me of that verse Christians always quote when things aren't going well. Romans 8:28. It says, 'And we know in all things God works for the good of those who love him, who have been called according to his purpose.'"

Something struck Jarrod the wrong way. "Whoa, say that again. It sounds as if it's not for everyone." Brad quoted the verse again.

"Yeah, doesn't it sound as if it's just for those who love God?"

Brad said, "Yeah, but that makes sense, right? God is going to work for the good of those who love him. The folks who believe, follow, and obey him. These are the folks he's going to work for."

The professor refocused their attention. "Brad's right, but the reason this verse relates to Isaiah 46 is because we see that God accomplishes his purposes and that his purposes are good for us."

Lauren seemed distant again, preoccupied. "What's wrong, Lauren?" asked MacGregor.

"Oh, I don't know. It's really hard to say." The group remained silent until she resumed. "I guess it's just that these verses tell me that God is working out the big, huge things in life. The big stuff God purposes are the things he does. But my life is not tied in to the big stuff. It's just me in my world at work and my family and my friends. For the sake of discussion, I'll agree that God is huge and mysterious as you say and that he has these big purposes that he accomplishes. Fine. He just seems so remote. It just doesn't seem to intersect with my reality."

MacGregor thought for a moment. "You know, Lauren, if God were just all-powerful and handling the big stuff, he wouldn't seem all that attractive to me either. Powerful but distant is no winning combination. That just makes him sound like my school principal who ran things with her long arm of the law. I would respect God. I would fear him.

But I wouldn't love him." He hesitated and then said deliberately, "I wouldn't feel the tender emotion of a child before his Father."

MacGregor looked intently into Lauren's eyes, and she sensed again that he somehow had insight into her life. It was her turn to feel exposed. She almost recoiled, but MacGregor looked at Brad and Jarrod as he continued.

"But you know what? I *do* feel love for God. Look at what Jesus says about his Father." MacGregor pulled the Bible across the table, and the pages quickly whispered under his skilled fingers. He turned the Bible around again to Lauren and asked, "What do you see here in Matthew 10:29?"

Lauren's eyes followed MacGregor's finger to the beginning of a verse. She said, "Are not two sparrows sold for a penny? Yet not one of them will fall to the ground apart from the will of your Father."

"Go on, through verse 31."

"And even the hairs of your head are numbered. So don't be afraid; you are worth more than many sparrows."

Lauren read and reread those last words several times to herself. *Could this be true? When God looks at me, does* he *really see me as having worth?*

She looked up into MacGregor's eyes, eyes filled with vitality and understanding and love. *Somehow he does know,* she thought. *He knows about me.*

"Lauren, God is not distant. He is not just handling the 'big stuff.' It's true that he governs the whole universe. Everything is in God's hand. But look at what his will is like—how does Jesus illustrate his Father's will?"

Jarrod said, "Something really cheap like sparrows are tied in to his will."

"Yes. What else?"

"He's got the hairs on our heads numbered."

"Yes, which in my case is a lot fewer hairs to keep track of than years ago. But are you getting this? Are you really hearing Jesus' words? He's telling you and me that the Father's will—the Father's governance—connects to something as cheap as a half-cent sparrow. What is hair worth? Is hair the big stuff in the world? No way. But he's even got our hairs numbered. And look how Jesus finishes: 'You are worth more than many sparrows.' This is amazing understatement! I love this. Why does Jesus tell us this? Jesus tells us this because *if* the Father's will encompasses stuff with little value, how much more does it encompass us who are worth more than many sparrows?"

Jarrod, Brad, and Lauren drank all this in. This was beautiful.

MacGregor continued, "I can summarize it this way. God's love for you is both *extravagant* and *meticulous.* It is *extravagant* in that he gives the best he has—his only Son—and it is *meticulous* in that he is concerned with even the hairs on our heads. When we think of God ruling the universe and our lives, we must remember that his governance reflects great love, extravagant and meticulous. Our God is a God worthy of being loved as well as feared, adored as well as revered."

Again the three were quiet, reflecting on this trove of provocative, enticing thought. After a minute or so Lauren said, "So does this help you with the war in Iraq? I guess if you really believed this stuff, you wouldn't be as worried about what's happening in the world."

"Excellent question, Lauren. Let me come back to Iraq in a minute because I want to put it in recent context. Think of masses of Americans in the weeks before 9/11—people apprehensive about the slumping economy; frivolity and superficiality characterized lots of pop culture, and many Americans went about their lives as though God does not exist.

"Then the terrorists struck. Americans recoiled in fear. Do you remember the expressions of need for God? Attendance spiked at houses of worship all over the country for one or two weeks. The media reported people repenting of all kinds of sins. Commentators announced the death of postmodernism and irony, as if that were a good thing. People prayed, waved flags, gathered together, spent time with families, and hoped God would get us out of this jam. God, who was not on many radar screens before 9/11, became the center of peoples' lives, and people implored him for help or demanded answers for how he could have failed us so badly in letting the suffering happen.

"Then what happened? President Bush served beautifully in many ways in the wake of the attack, no question. He did a great job in rallying the nation. However, the president suggested two startling things: one, that we needed to go back to normal; and two, which was related, we needed to shop, to consume, to get the economy moving.

"I couldn't believe it. I desperately didn't want to get back to normal. *Status quo* before 9/11 entailed a selfish, God-dishonoring way of life for many. Personally, I believe a lot of the *de facto* atheism that we see in Americans' everyday lives, including evangelical Christians' lives, arises from this consumption mentality. We anesthetize ourselves by our consuming, especially the consuming quest for comfort. So just when we've been jarred into seeing reality for what it is and seeing the falsity of our prior frivolous existence—as we are repenting and seeking God—we are told to scramble back into normality and consumerism.

"We were comfortable and hardly God centered before 9/11. The crisis terrified us; then slowly we resumed our consumerism and superficiality. Then the war clouds with Iraq began, and the country got freaked out again. Notice, all of this roller-coaster movement is on our side. God hasn't moved. Reality never changed; only our perceptions of our safety rose and fell and rose again.

"Now, back to your question, Lauren. Yes, knowing that God accomplishes his purposes, that he declares the end from the beginning, that he works out everything in conformity to his will, that he loves us meticulously and extravagantly, gives me hope and peace. My faith and allegiance emphatically do not repose primarily in the United States of America. My faith is in the Lord Almighty, who has my first allegiance.

I do have a certain amount of trust that Americans in all walks of life will work well to stamp out terrorism, and I *hope* that we will also work for justice, kindness, and righteousness on the earth, though the jury is still out on that count. In terms of allegiance as a citizen of the United States, I have allegiance to our country. But my first and best citizenship, and where my faith lies, is in Christ and his kingdom."

Again the group reflected silently on MacGregor's account for a bit before Brad spoke up. "Professor MacGregor, this is really amazing. I can't tell you what this means to me. I came in here stressed about my meeting and, in a sense, my entire life, and you've given me the best lunch I've had in a long time. Who would have thought?

"Everything today has happened right on schedule."

Brad smiled as the *schedule* word came back in the conversation. How different it seemed now. "So you think God had me meet you at church, and introduce you to the group, and Lauren spill her drink and everything?"

"I am convinced of it, my friend."

"For what purpose though?"

"Well, just what you said—that this was the best lunch you've had in a long time. All I did was ask some questions and then open up the Scriptures, and then you asked some questions. I think the Father accomplished some of his meticulous purposes today."

Brad smiled, nodding his head. "You're right. You're absolutely right. But how did you know to ask those questions and bring up these Bible passages?"

"Well, I've taught the doctrines of the Christian faith for decades. Every issue I've encountered in my own life and in the lives of others relates to the teachings—or doctrines—of the Bible. The real and personal issues of my life, and how I respond to them, are utterly tied in to Christian doctrine."

"Really?" asked Jarrod. "I've always heard that doctrine was irrelevant and impractical. As much as I love philosophy, I keep it strictly separate from my spiritual life. I've seen some who get into doctrine become dead and heartless Christians. I've always believed that the real stuff is loving Jesus with your heart and loving others. When you see how much we are into loving people and how dead the rigid doctrine people are at other churches, you can understand why *doctrine* is pretty much a bad word at my church."

"Fair enough. I agree that a number of people who are into doctrine and the cognitive aspects of Christianity have calloused hearts. You can stop following Jesus and stop having affection for him and still win arguments about doctrine. It's true that too many Christians are this way. I have to ask you: was our discussion helpful to you today?"

"Well, yeah, it was amazing. I love this stuff, and I like how you do it."

"Jarrod, without ever mentioning the actual word, I've been teaching you what theologians call the 'doctrine of providence.' What has been so meaningful to you today is the doctrine of providence. Look at how you felt *before* you learned this doctrine and think about how you feel *now* that you know these truths."

Jarrod still had a hard time swallowing the idea that doctrine in general was useful. "Yeah, but this providence stuff is just one thing that happens to relate to what we're dealing with right now. I've seen, in my own personal experience, too many dead, rigid Christians who were obsessed with doctrine. I *know* these people, and I'm having a hard time buying that the other doctrines are this practical."

"Actually, they are. As I said before, every issue in my life and the lives of others relates to doctrine. Not knowing doctrinal truth can impair us, and knowing it can really, really bless us. These are not idle words or irrelevant truth; doctrine is truth for *life*."

"I've never heard it be this relevant. I hope you've got more of this," said Brad.

"Absolutely!" exclaimed the professor. "You have no idea how much wonderful doctrine there is that relates to the core of our everyday lives. Teachings are the map that Jesus gave us to help us make it home."

"So doctrines are teachings?" asked a puzzled Lauren.

"Yes. Actually the same Greek word in the New Testament is trans-lated sometimes as *doctrine* and sometimes as *teaching.* The teachings of the Bible are doctrines, and I promise you that the doctrines of God are supremely practical to our lives."

A middle-aged man walked in with a suit jacket on a hanger. Peering around the coffee shop, he saw the group in the corner. "Mac," he called out, "here's your friend's jacket." He approached them with a smile. "Young man, this must be yours."

Brad stood up, reached for the jacket, and said, "Thank you." MacGregor introduced them all. "Brad, Lauren, Jarrod, this is a dear friend of mine, Bob Martin, the owner of the cleaners. Bob, please meet Brad Masterson, Lauren Fontenot, and Jarrod Holcomb." As they shook hands with Martin, the professor said, "Bob, we just had a very pleasant visit."

Martin smiled broadly. "So ole Mac's been at you, has he? Well, you don't know this yet, but when Mac becomes your friend, you get a best friend for life. Mac is the most loyal, devoted, caring, and *infuriating* friend I've got."

MacGregor chuckled and said, "Bob and I go way back. We've gone through a lot of life together, and he's always there to pull some prank at my expense. I get him back occasionally."

"Great to meet you guys. Wish I could stay and chat, but I've got to take care of a few things at the shop. Have a great day." And Bob Martin headed for the door.

MacGregor turned back and surveyed them and said, "This is prob-ably a good time to stop. I know you've got things to do, even if it's a slow day.

"But I've got an idea for next time. Instead of meeting here, let's take a road trip. We got into something last time about the Grand

Canyon and worship, and there are some other Christian beliefs that relate to all that. What do you say? Up for something different?"

"Depends," said Brad. "In principle I'm game, but as you know, it's really hard for me to know because the demands on me at the office are unpredictable. And, if you don't mind my asking, what do you have in mind?"

"I'm not exactly sure yet, but Brad E-mailed me the contact info for each of you last month, so I will take responsibility for coordinating this time. I'm thinking Saturday evening in general, though. Is that a good time?"

"That's normally a time I blow off steam by going out to eat and dance, but I'm intrigued by the idea of a road trip. As soon as you know what you want to do, let me know," said Lauren.

Jarrod concurred. "It's a good night to go out, but you know I love this, and I'm interested in what you've got up your sleeve. I'm in."

MacGregor agreed. "Sounds good. Brad, we'll hope your schedule permits. Thank you all again. I really enjoy being with you. This has been wonderful."

They shook hands and bid one another a great rest of the week. As they exited the coffeehouse for the street, each wondered what the Saturday get-together had in store.

Chapter 7

Creation Speaks

JARROD SWUNG BY THE RICE HOTEL where Lauren waited outside. She waved and smiled as he drew up to the curb in his red Ford Explorer. He popped the locks and returned the smile as she opened the door. She wasted no time placing her beach chair and bag in the backseat before climbing in the front passenger seat and fiddling with the seat belt. For the first time Jarrod noticed the killer light-blue sundress that showed off her impressive legs and said, "Wow." These days Lauren wore professional attire most of the occasions when they were together, which was usually at the coffeehouse, so he rarely saw her at her cute, sexy best as he had at UT.

"You like?" she asked flirtatiously. Lauren knew how to torture the guys in her orbit.

Jarrod shook his head helplessly. "Mmm, yeah, I like."

"You trimmed your hair!"

"Well, it was getting annoying in the eyes. So I had the barber clean it up a bit."

"Jarrod, it looks good. You've got your wakeboard thing going again. So wild." She laughed, partly at him, partly with him. She was in high spirits, and even charismatic Jarrod could be played when she was in this mode.

"So are you excited to be going down to the beach?" she asked.

"You know it. I'm sky-high. I can't wait to get away from the city for a few hours. I'm so glad the professor suggested this."

"Me too! I can't believe how excited I am. It's obviously been too long since I got out of town. And I am so curious about what we're going to talk about. He's been pretty fascinating in our conversations."

"He really has," Jarrod agreed. "I can't figure him out, but I just know that it's OK. I've never encountered anyone like him, but I think he's utterly cool. He's certainly making me think about what I believe."

"Me too. Sometimes it's uncomfortable because he's challenging my personal beliefs, but overall it's been pretty fun and interesting."

Their conversation turned to their escapades from the previous night as Jarrod drove up the I-45 ramp and turned the Explorer south toward Galveston.

† † †

Jarrod and Lauren pulled into the parking lot adjacent to a stretch of West Beach, and they could see the older gentleman standing on the sand facing the surf. At this five o'clock hour a cool breeze began to kick up and blow wisps of MacGregor's hair as it chased away the remnant heat, which still slightly simmered even in mid-October afternoons on the Texas Gulf Coast. The sun, well into its languid descent, sent farewell beams reflecting off the clouds in a pinkish-purple panorama. As Lauren and Jarrod started to open their doors, the power of nature's beauty arrested their efforts. They both just sat in the Explorer and stared for a minute or so before they noticed MacGregor waving. "We better go," Jarrod said. "He's waiting on us." After they emerged from the vehicle, clutching their towels and beach chairs, they schussed their feet through the sand toward MacGregor's blanket.

"Hello, Professor," Lauren called out gaily. In spite of her trepidation about his seeming ability to guess things about her, she could tell that he genuinely cared for her. He was so gentle. And for an old professor, pretty with it too. He was clad in new athletic sandals, khaki shorts, and a golf shirt. He looked the picture of beach cool, she thought. Well, beach cool for an older adult.

"Hello, Lauren. Great to see you again." He hugged her fondly with one arm in a side embrace and then pulled in Jarrod with the other arm for similar treatment. "Jarrod, my boy, it is good to see you. How was the trip down?"

"Great. Getting away from the library and getting out here to this"—Jarrod gestured around him in a circle—"makes life worth living. This is so beautiful! I *love* it!"

"Absolutely," Lauren exulted. "It is *gorgeous* out here!" She kicked up some sand and raised her hands to the skies. They all felt dramatically free just being out in the evening. Traffic, work, and a thousand details from incomprehensibly complex lives created burdens, conscious and unconscious, that weighed them down—but not here. It was as if crossing the boundary from parking lot to the sand made their worries and to-do lists take flight.

The trio fell silent, again looking intently into the waves and colorful clouds. A long while elapsed before Jarrod broke the silence.

"This is the best. I feel so alive here. But," he grinned, "I'm so hungry!"

"Not to worry," MacGregor said, "I think we're covered on food."

"Martha Stewart, eat your heart out!" exclaimed Lauren. "I didn't even see this spread. You brought all this? Good gracious!"

Near them lay a large picnic blanket topped with a classic American feast. Tupperware lids covered fried chicken, potato salad, corn on the cob, and deviled eggs. A large blue cooler revealed bottled water, iced tea, soft drinks, and, in the cooler's "dry box," a homemade pecan pie. "Where did you get all this?" asked Jarrod.

"Marilynn, my wife, is hosting a party tonight for some of the women she mentors, and I told her I would vacate the premises in return for food." He winked. "Apparently, that was an offer she could not refuse. To be honest, Marilynn loves cooking for folks and throwing parties. She's heard all about you guys, and she wanted to say a warm hello by sending a little love in a basket. Marilynn is something, isn't she?"

"I'll say," Jarrod offered enthusiastically. "There's enough for two of me!"

"Well, it does seem like a lot, but we thought Brad was coming. He called to say he's going to miss the picnic out here, but he's going to meet us at the bookstore on the Strand later. He's working late tonight."

"His loss," said Jarrod. "What on earth could his bosses be needing from him on Saturday night? He's been working till ten or eleven most nights this week. That's the sad downside to investment banking at the associate level. They just jack him around for all these tasks. You should hear him tell stories about the silly editing process he goes through with vice presidents and directors when they're putting together a deal. It's hilarious, except Brad misses out on life." Jarrod spoke with passionate empathy for his friend.

Lauren pondered, for the umpteenth time, how similar her own life sounded to what Jarrod just described about Brad's—except for about 30 percent less salary. Inwardly she kicked herself again. She hated that she worked as hard as he did, doing a lot of the same financial research, for so much less money and prestige.

The professor broke the sympathy party. "OK friends, get out your beach chairs and let's dig in. If you don't mind, I'd like to offer a prayer of thanks to the Lord for this food."

† † †

Some forty minutes later Jarrod patted his stomach and announced he was stuffed. Lauren and the professor agreed, and after they wiped their hands, their active conversation began to subside. The sun lingered near the end of its arc, promising light for a little while longer, while the faint blue skies and the breeze finally seduced them into silence.

After a bit MacGregor said, "God does good work, don't you agree?" Lauren and Jarrod could see joy and reverence in his countenance. Lauren chuckled, endeared to this man's unaffected love for his God. He might be too religious for her own liking, but they certainly didn't come any more real.

Jarrod nodded his head. "The best. And in my travels I've seen the Swiss Alps, waterfalls, deserts. Everywhere you go, you can see God's work."

"Travels?"

"Yeah. My parents took us on vacations. Even though they tended to ruin the experience, I got to see some amazing things. And when I was taking time off before school, you know, the summer before starting college, I backpacked around. I was so glad I was a Christian because I could really appreciate God in what I saw."

"That's interesting, Jarrod. I had no idea you'd had such terrific travels. How about you, Lauren? What do you think when you see all this?"

"Well, I do agree that this is God's work. Maybe not your God, but as I told you when we first met, the god I believe in is *in* everything." She grinned mischievously.

"Do you want a playful response or a serious one?" asked MacGregor, eyes twinkling as usual.

"Oh, playful for sure. But I suspect I might learn something if you give me the serious one. OK, what is your take?"

"Lauren, are we still operating under the same conditions? We talked before about my telling you the Christian story. You've told us about your god, and I've told you some about the Christian God. What sparked the idea to come down to Galveston was our talking about your going to the Grand Canyon with your friend. If you're OK with this, I'd like to continue telling you more about the Christian story."

"Sure. This has been fun. I've sort of just suspended disbelief for a bit. I mean, I've been pretty clear that I don't believe the Bible or the

Christian religion. But I'm learning a lot, and you've definitely gone about this differently from anyone else in my life. So, yeah, go ahead. I'm enjoying learning."

"OK, great. Thank you. To begin, responding to what you said about God's being in everything, definitely God's *character* can be seen in everything he makes, so in that sense I would agree that God is in all of creation. I guess I would reply to you that I don't believe he is actually *in* trees and mountains and waves, but I believe reflections of God are. So, right now, when I look at the ocean at sunset, I 'see' God."

"What do you mean, Professor?"

"One of my favorite psalms talks about creation and what creation 'speaks' about the Lord. I'm aware that pulling out the Bible at a picnic might be odd, but it's actually why I wanted us to meet down here this time. But only with your permission." As in their two previous meetings, MacGregor had his Bible handy, this time in one of the picnic baskets. Jarrod and Lauren looked at each other and shrugged their shoulders. "Sure," said Jarrod. "That's fine."

MacGregor found Psalm 19 and asked, "Lauren, would you please read verses 1–4?"

"OK." She shook her hair in the breeze and rocked forward in her chair. "'The heavens declare the glory of God; the skies proclaim the work of his hands. Day after day they pour forth speech; night after night they display knowledge. There is no speech or language where their voice is not heard. Their voice goes out into all the earth, their words to the ends of the world.'"

Lauren looked up at MacGregor. "I really like that. See, we do agree on some things."

"Of course. So what do you think this passage is saying?" asked the professor.

She looked down again at the Bible. "I love the idea that nature communicates. That is such a brilliant thought. We think of humans as being these advanced communicative creatures, and we marvel at our sophistication. Practicing law, for example. Everything I *do* is about communication—communicating with clients, other associates, partners, secretaries, financial services folks."

Lauren paused, thinking, and began again, "And we are so image conscious these days. We're really aware of the power of symbol and image to communicate. Just look at MTV or commercials on TV. We marvel at our sophisticated communication when it comes to marketing, but I don't know if people stop to think that *nature itself* communicates. At least, I don't. So when I read this—whatever you called it . . ."

"Psalm," MacGregor answered.

"This psalm," she continued, "I think it is a really clever metaphor. It makes me stop and think rather than just fly by it."

"And what does nature communicate?"

Lauren read the passage again. "It looks as if it's saying that the skies are communicating God's prowess as Creator. Yes?"

"Yes," said MacGregor, as Jarrod indicated his agreement. "But it's not just that they report something about God. The skies are not sending out a memo about the contractor. The skies themselves are declaring by their very nature. The composition of the sky itself says something about God."

"But it says the heavens declare his glory. That might not be a memo, but it *is* a report."

"If it was just the first line, I might agree with you. But Hebrew poetry, and the psalms are the poems of the ancient Hebrews, is characterized by its couplets. The second line of a couplet qualifies the first line. Sometimes the second line complements the first, enlarges the meaning, restricts the meaning, or explains the first line by coming at the meaning in a different way. What does the second line say?"

"The skies proclaim the work of his hands."

"And how does that relate to the first line about declaring God's glory?"

"I see what you're saying. The skies, since they are the work of his hands. OK, it's saying that the skies, by their own greatness, show how great God is because he made them. They are great, and that shows the greatness of the Maker."

"Yes!" exclaimed MacGregor.

Finally, Lauren thought, *we're actually on the same page for once.*

"And what else does it say?"

Again Lauren's eyes went to the Bible. As she read, MacGregor glanced over at Jarrod and beamed. Jarrod could see the professor and Lauren were enjoying a special moment, and he appeared content to stay out of the way.

Lauren said, "As I said before, I like the way it says the skies 'pour forth speech.' I just think that is an awesome picture. When I read that phrase, it evokes images of Niagara Falls. It's this picture of overflowing, cascading information. Tons and tons of information pouring out."

MacGregor asked, "And what is the content of that information?"

"Hmmm," Lauren considered this more carefully. "Well, the glory of God. And the work of his hands suggests that he is this really amazing Builder-Architect. And because this," she gestured in the direction of the disappearing disk in the horizon, "is *so* beautiful, I guess the information is that *God* is beautiful."

"It's like when I took an art history class," she continued. "I remember we discussed the lives and personalities of artists like Leonardo da Vinci and Michelangelo. We agreed there was something in these men of rare beauty and greatness. So, if the skies and all of nature are pouring forth speech about the work of God's hands, then he must be at *least* as magical and wonderful as what he makes."

Jarrod and MacGregor stared at her until a gust of wind blew some of their leftover napkins. Lauren jumped up. "I'll get 'em. We can't litter after talking about God in nature." She jogged off to chase the napkins that bounded away with more breeze.

MacGregor and Jarrod now looked at each other. "Jarrod, she's remarkable, isn't she? But I guess you've known that for years. I marvel at how much Lauren understands."

"It is amazing. She's always been phenomenally intelligent, but the one area where she is not respectful of others is religion, or at least Christianity. I've never seen her be so relaxed or open or whatever as she is with you."

"Do you know why she's so hostile?"

"No. Brad and I have asked over the years, but she would just talk about judgmental Christians. I always assumed it was because she parties and was angry at Christians' judgment of her lifestyle. Compared to most people, Lauren's pretty tame and traditional, but compared to intense Christians, especially Brad's type, I guess she's a bit wild. As far as I know, that's where the anger comes from. She doesn't take much static from anyone."

They could see Lauren snag the napkins, and then she tramped over to a distant trash can to deposit them.

"Interesting. Over the years I've become accustomed to the Lord's using me to connect with Christians and non-Christians alike, but I've never seen someone not steeped in the faith pick up so quickly on the right things."

Jarrod nodded. "Yeah, I know. She's always been supersmart and cuts to the chase in a debate. But I guess you're right; this is different. Even though I've seen her strut her stuff for a long time, this is pretty special. She's really getting what you are saying."

"You never know, but I wonder if Lauren might overcome her objections to Christianity. She's so close in some ways yet undeniably and self-consciously faraway in others."

They watched her jog back and rearrange herself in her beach chair.

"So what do you think about what I said? Do you agree that if a beautiful work of art by da Vinci shows the beauty of his genius, how much more does all this beauty show the creative genius of God?"

"Lauren, I don't think I could say it any better," MacGregor said like a proud father. "You've got it. Nature reveals God because it shows his power, his creativity, his genius and beauty. One more thing

I want to get at from this passage, though, before we move on. Where is this information communicated? How pervasively is this information distributed?"

Lauren read the lines again and said, "Everywhere. This goes along with what you and I were saying about our respective divinities last time. While I think God is in everything and everybody, you say God is present everywhere. 'There's nowhere one can go to get away from him,' I think is how you put it. So I guess the skies and nature are everywhere pouring out the information."

"That's right," said the professor. "And thus the Lord inundates the whole world with information about himself. Regardless of geography, language, society. The whole world has access to this information about God and thus information about his character."

Lauren and Jarrod nodded.

"So we can say that God has revealed himself *generally*. This is what Christian theologians call 'general revelation.' That is, God has revealed information or knowledge about himself generally through creation. The peoples of the world have knowledge of God impinging on their senses. Information via creation barrages folks every day, all day."

Again Lauren and Jarrod nodded.

"But this brings up a problem. Lauren, what was your reaction to the Grand Canyon? Remember, you said you felt small; you felt awe. It was a humbling experience. You wanted to celebrate. But not everyone reacts that way, and that is the problem."

"Why is that a problem?" inquired Lauren.

"Well, when we encounter a person, don't you think we should respond to that person appropriately? And when that person is God, the appropriate response is adoration, humility, and worship. If we don't, then we act unrighteously."

The last word brought Jarrod and Lauren up short. *Unrighteously* was so jarring. That was too much. MacGregor could read the disagreement on their faces, so again he directed their attention to the Bible.

"Here. Let's look at Romans 1:18–20." He found the place and nudged the Bible toward Lauren while holding his finger in place to keep the wind from blowing the pages.

She picked it up and read, "'The wrath of God is being revealed from heaven against all the godlessness and wickedness of men who suppress the truth by their wickedness, since what may be known about God is plain to them, because God has made it plain to them. For since the creation of the world God's invisible qualities—his eternal power and divine nature—have been clearly seen, being understood from what has been made, so that men are without excuse.'"

Lauren laid the Bible down and said, "I don't like that at all. You see, *this* is the problem I have with Christians. This is *so* offensive. How can you believe all of that about wrath and unrighteousness? God isn't like that at all. He is about *love*."

Lauren, like most people, was complex in her makeup. At any given moment her need to please people could give way to her deeply rooted feelings about tolerance and being judged. In five minutes the people-pleaser mentality might come to the fore again, but at this moment her feelings and capable intellect made her a bit feisty.

"Lauren, God is love, no question. You're right about that. Let me see if we can de-escalate this a bit and come at it another way. Would that be all right with you?" The deeply creased smile lines again animated MacGregor's face.

Lauren's frustration intensified. She thought, *Why did he have to be so gentle? How can I say no?*

Lauren felt off balance and dissatisfied, but she couldn't put her finger on it. MacGregor had a way of taking the toxin out of her frustration, but what she didn't put together was that this conversational detox kept her from giving full vent to her feelings at the moment. Of course, if she had thought about all this consciously, she would probably agree that giving full vent to her feelings had caused regret numerous times in her life. Still, the full-vent approach at least left a person with a sense of immediate satisfaction, and MacGregor's deft intervention deprived her of that.

"I guess," she replied, visibly irritated.

"Do you get angry?" asked the professor.

Lauren just looked at him, but she didn't answer.

"For example," MacGregor continued, "does the Bible make you angry? Or do you get angry when you see intolerance?"

"Obviously, intolerance makes me angry," she replied impatiently.

"Is that OK?"

"What do you mean?"

"Is it OK for you to get angry when you see intolerance?"

"Of course! Professor, most people are clued in to the fact that intolerance is wrong. When people are racist or prejudiced or intolerant, they're wrong. So, yeah, I do get angry when I see that kind of behavior."

"Are you intolerant of other peoples' intolerance?"

"What?" snapped Lauren, but she intuitively sensed he had her on the ropes again.

"You say you legitimately get angry at peoples' intolerance. So I assume you are intolerant of intolerance."

"*I* am not intolerant. You're twisting this all around, and now *I'm* the bad guy? I'm talking about *those people* who judge others who are different from them. People who exclude them or call them names or look down their noses. *That's* what I mean by intolerance."

"So the people you like are tolerant of others. The folks you're closest to—your best friends—all share this common outlook of tolerance."

"Yes."

"And the people you don't like are the intolerant ones. These are people who make you angry. Lauren, you say you don't like people who judge others for being different. You say you're the same as your friends—tolerant.

"Thus, the people you don't like are the ones who are different from you and your friends. But you end up doing the same thing to others.

You judge intolerant people; you think they are wrong. You are intolerant of their behavior. So you are intolerant of intolerance."

"You're twisting my words. I'm not *saying* that. I see what you're trying to do, but I'm talking about people who judge other religions as being wrong, or tell people that gays and lesbians are wrong, or discriminate against African-Americans."

"Lauren, then you're not against intolerance in general, you're just against specific examples of intolerance like racism."

"No, I *am* against intolerance in general! And that's what I mean by intolerance—gay bashing, telling consenting adults that sex outside of marriage is wrong, and saying that one's religion is the only right way."

"Lauren, I don't think you see what you're doing. You are taking a word—*intolerance*—and you're *redefining* it so that it only applies to the moral positions that *you* embrace. *Intolerance* is a word meaning disapproval of something that crosses over a boundary. You are using *intolerance* in such a way as to limit it to *only* the cultural issues that matter to you. But tolerance and intolerance apply to any number of issues and positions. If you were *truly* tolerant in an *absolute* sense, you would tolerate *any* and *every*thing, including those who are racists. But you are intolerant of racism because you think it is wrong to be intolerant of other races."

"Right! I *do* think it's wrong."

"And you still don't see that because you think racism is wrong you are intolerant of racism?"

For the first time the light dawned on Lauren. She had used the word *intolerance* for so many years in so many discussions, and she had believed her spiel on intolerance so passionately, that she had never been aware that she had identified the word only with specific issues like racism, gay bashing, and religion bashing.

"Yes, I'm starting to see what you mean. If I am opposed to anything, I am intolerant of that thing."

"So back to what I said originally, you are intolerant of intolerance."

"I still don't *like* that. It makes me sound like a hypocrite."

"Remember our discussion about truth last month? I talked about how most people are loyal to family or friends, but I strive to be loyal to truth. Usually those don't conflict, but when they do, I try not to bend or change a principle just so a friend can feel like his action is OK. Truth is not a matter of mere preference. It's not about whether we *like* something; it's about whether the statement is *accurate*. Regardless of how you *feel* about the phrase, 'intolerant of intolerance,' doesn't it accurately describe your position?"

Lauren sighed, and her body language signaled her reluctant agreement. As in previous discussions with MacGregor, this proved so difficult and frustrating. The realization that he saw the whole world *completely* differently than she did continued to astonish her. How could two people see things so differently?

"Lauren, we're far afield from the Romans 1 passage that began this. My point in asking about whether you get angry at things and asking whether you are intolerant of intolerance is to highlight the fact that you feel legitimate anger at people when they behave wrongly. And I agree with you that *it is wrong* to be racist, to bash gay people or other religions. I am intolerant of those things too. Thus, I would say that in some positions intolerance is wrong, and in other positions intolerance is right. It depends on the issue. For example, I'm intolerant of anti-Semitism. If I hear someone making anti-Semitic statements, I get angry. But I'm tolerant of different perspectives in politics. I tolerate Republicans, Democrats, and Independents and think all their candidates have the right to try to turn their different platforms into laws. I may disagree with certain positions, but I tolerate them."

Lauren nodded.

"So here's the crux of the matter. We all agree that we can get angry and oppose people who do evil. Certain issues and behaviors offend your standards, and certain issues and behaviors offend my standards. The question that gets us back to Romans 1 is this: Does God have standards?"

Lauren and Jarrod looked at MacGregor, then at each other. Jarrod felt just as uncomfortable as Lauren about the use of words like *wrath* and *unrighteousness*. He also saw God almost exclusively as a God of love. But the way MacGregor phrased the question, it did seem natural to him that God would have standards. And his studies in philosophy had him trained to see the logical conclusion—a God that had standards would be displeased by someone breaking those standards. Still, *wrath* seemed way over the line to Jarrod.

For her part, Lauren felt suddenly wary because she had already experienced being on the wrong side of MacGregor's questions. She felt trapped. If she said yes, he would go somewhere with her yes, though Lauren didn't immediately see where that path would lead. If she said no, then he would say God approves of everything, including the Holocaust. She remembered this vein of thought from their last conversation at Common Grounds.

"I don't know." Not only did that seem safe; it was absolutely honest.

MacGregor smiled and said, "Fair enough. I think God does have standards, and just as you and I get angry at injustice, so does God. The issue is not that God gets angry—I'm *grateful* he does. If he didn't get angry at injustice, when helpless people are slaughtered, for example, he would be heartless. Look, you and I and everyone else—we're far from perfect. We make mistakes all the time. And yet we can have moral outrage at others who do wrong. How much more can a holy, perfect God, who never makes a mistake, get angry at injustice? His wrath is not a blemish on his character but a brilliant jewel that shows God is both *just* and *passionate* about justice."

Jarrod nodded cautiously, waiting to see where this was going before he gave full approval, and Lauren had to agree that this did make sense. It was just hard to express it in the same terms that MacGregor had used because all of her life she and her friends had mocked the Christian God. Or at least in high school they had mocked the God they saw portrayed in Hawthorne's *Scarlet Letter* and that scary sermon clip in their English anthology book. She remembered being speechless with fury at that paragraph from Jonathan Edwards's "Sinners in the Hands of an Angry God." How often she and her friends had used that sermon as an example of why Christians were sick, twisted people. So here was this verse in Romans saying God *did* have wrath toward wicked people, and it just did not agree with her. However, MacGregor's reasoning was compelling. She got angry at certain things, so it made sense that God could get angry legitimately as well. It felt like an out-of-body experience assenting to the professor's point. He might be right, but it still sounded funny—actually inappropriate—to say that God was wrathful.

"OK," she said at last.

"If you will recall, we were talking about Psalm 19 and your Grand Canyon experience. You were absolutely right about what Psalm 19 means. Through God's creation, information about the Creator pours out all over the world to every culture. There is no place where people live that God's creation is not communicating tons of information about him. And, as you agreed, the correct response to this is worship. You feel awe, humility, gladness. It is the proper response to God's general reve-lation of himself."

MacGregor paused. "But here is the problem. Romans 1 tells us that not everyone does respond to God the right way. God *does* have stan-dards, and he *does* legitimately get angry when people discard the in-formation pouring out of creation and instead worship beings other than the true God. It is the height of disrespect. Does that make sense?"

Jarrod, as he had all evening, agreed. Lauren, though, wavered. "It makes sense, yes, but I am not *persuaded.*" Picking up the Bible, she read the Romans passage aloud again. "'The wrath of God is being revealed from heaven against all the godlessness and wickedness of men who suppress the truth by their wickedness, since what may be known about God is plain to them, because God has made it plain to them. For since the creation of the world God's invisible qualities—his eternal power and divine nature—have been clearly seen, being understood from what has been made, so that men are without excuse.'

"So, this is saying that God has revealed himself—what you were calling general revelation—to everybody. Creation shows God's qualities, so in essence, using the words from the verse, God has made himself plainly known to them."

"Yes, you've nailed it again, Lauren," said the professor. "Thus, people don't have what?"

"An excuse. But why would they need an excuse?"

"When you were threatened with punishment as a child, did you ever try to get out of it with some kind of excuse?"

"Of course! I was pretty good at it too!" Lauren flashed a devilish grin.

"Exactly. People who reject the information end up incurring God's wrath. Instead of being humble and pure and worshipful toward the Lord, these people manufacture their own gods, or they live apart from the moral order embedded in God's creation. God calls this behavior—either manufacturing other gods or living apart from his moral will—unrighteousness. In this passage in Romans, Paul is sort of imagining a time when these wicked people get wind of the coming punishment, so they try to come up with excuses to get out of it. But God says that they are without excuse; there is no excuse for abandoning morality and worship of the Lord because what they needed to know to live morally and worship the Lord is being poured out in creation."

"So God is angry at them for starting other religions? Isn't that small and petty of God?"

"Well, some might see it that way, but listen to verse 25 in Romans 1. It says, 'They exchanged the truth of God for a lie, and worshiped and served created things rather than the Creator—who is forever praised.' You see, wicked people *suppress* the knowledge of God that is generally revealed to the whole world, and instead of worshiping the God who made all this beauty, they worship the created things themselves. That is not only offensive to the greatest being in the universe, but it is also a lie. No created thing is *worthy* of worship; the Creator *alone* is."

Lauren replied, "I see your point. It makes sense, definitely. But there is a strange ring to this. I have this vague sense that I don't like this."

"Can you ascertain why?" asked MacGregor.

"I'm not sure. I think, if this is true, then this undermines the idea that all religions are equal, which is something that I definitely believe. No one should say their religion or their culture is better than another. And this verse makes it sound like any religion that doesn't worship God is wicked and that the people will receive wrath."

"Lauren, you're right about the implications of this verse. And I do want to explore this topic of *pluralism* with you. It is relevant to this discussion, but it also gets us offtrack just a bit. So, if you will agree, I'd like to explore pluralism at another time."

"Pluralism? What the heck is that?" asked Lauren.

For the first time in a long while Jarrod spoke up. "Pluralism is the idea of multiple religions or philosophies. In other words, pluralism is not singular, meaning one, but plural, meaning many. If you're a pluralist, you believe that the presence of the many different perspectives means you can't say one is right."

Lauren said, "Well, I guess I'm a pluralist. I think it's arrogant to say, 'My religion is right, and everyone else is going to hell.'"

Jarrod agreed, "Yeah, I admit it sounds uncool and close-minded to say your view is the only one that's true or right. But pluralism also has its own problems. In one philosophy class we discussed this whole issue and how it relates to political theory. Pluralism relates to the idea of democracy and values that citizens disagree about.

"Like the abortion issue," he continued. "In class we debated how your worldview influences your values and what you think should be laws. In fact, I had to write a paper about this very thing. In the U.S.

there used to be more agreement that Jewish and Christian moral values should be the underlying basis of our laws. While not everyone was a Christian and while the United States was not a 'Christian nation,' (Jarrod made the quotation signs with his hands) there really was widespread cultural agreement that the Bible was the basis for morality. Now there are *lots* of competing worldviews, and that's why we have so much fighting in politics. As I said, the abortion issue is a prime example. The problem for democracy is that you've got this pluralism—all these different worldviews—and which one gets to have its values become law? Who wins?"

MacGregor leaned back on the picnic blanket and said, "Jarrod, what can I say? That is an excellent summary of the issue. And it's true; many folks today are pluralists, maybe even most. I would love to revisit this topic at some other time. But for now it really will get us away from our topic before we finish it. I would like to highlight one other thing about the doctrine of general revelation before we pack up. It's getting pretty dark, so we need to get out of here while we still have a shred of light. But the last important thing about general revelation is that God has revealed himself to us in our fellow humans. You, Lauren, and you, Jarrod, are examples of God's self-revelation."

Lauren laughed, and, imitating a Hollywood starlet, said, "My friends tell me I'm *divine.*"

Jarrod laughed, too, and Lauren suspected his gaze and smile showed he inwardly agreed. Nice.

MacGregor said it: "Lauren, you *are* . . . in a sense. Literally, in a *sense.* One of the great Christian theologians of all time, John Calvin, said God created humans with a *sensus divinitatis.* This means 'sense of the divine.' God has implanted us with something of himself. The result is that humans long and yearn for connection with God. Whether people worship the Lord or whether they craft idols and worship them as their gods, the sense of the divine engraved on each of us propels us to worship. Also the *sensus divinitatis* means that humans have an internal, rudimentary knowledge of morality, such as 'don't kill' and 'don't steal.' Across cultures, across time, human societies have reflected these moral laws that are written on their hearts."

Aha, thought Lauren, *a hole in his thinking.* "But doesn't this contradict the passage in Romans about wickedness?"

"Excellent question, Lauren. You're a talented theologian. Please explain how *you* think it poses a contradiction."

"Well, you say God has implanted this divine sense in each of us, and it makes us yearn for him and gives us these internal moral laws. On the other hand, Romans says people suppress the knowledge of God and worship the wrong things, and so they get nailed with God's wrath. That seems like a contradiction to me."

Jarrod piped up. "Well, not exactly. A contradiction is when two statements are opposite each other. Or when two statements are put forth but they exclude the possibility of the other."

Lauren raised her eyebrows. "English?"

"Come on, Lawyer Lauren. You're supposed to know this. Where were you at law school the day they taught logic?" Her look told him to drop the attitude, so he hastened an "OK, OK. Well, the formal definition we learned in logic is this: A cannot be A and non-A at the same time in the same sense. The common example is a woman cannot be pregnant and not pregnant at the same time. And what you just said about the sense of God in each of us and the Romans 1 passage is not technically a contradiction. I agree that something sounds funny or off about what the professor is saying, but the statements are not technically a contradiction."

MacGregor smiled and looked at Lauren, who also smiled. *Impressive,* she thought. She loved it when Jarrod flexed his intellect.

"But you do see the problem?" she inquired of Jarrod.

"Yeah, something sounds amiss. What do you say, Professor?"

"You have highlighted something important. The doctrine of general revelation says that knowledge of God pours forth through creation, which includes both nature and human beings created with the *sensus divinitatis.* Thus, we humans have knowledge of God, his character, and his moral law written on our hearts. But humans *suppress* that knowledge through their wickedness. Humans repeatedly run away from God, and instead of worshiping him and building their lives around the God revealed generally, they build their lives around themselves or around created things. The result is that they receive God's wrath."

Jarrod contemplated this arrangement. "What are you saying then? I thought we could see God through nature and worship him. I mean, I never knew this doctrine of general revelation in a formal sense, but I agree with it. And now you're saying that everyone's doomed in *spite* of general revelation?"

"I wouldn't put it *quite* that way, but, yes. General revelation is not enough because our hearts are darkened, which is what Romans 1:21 says. To be saved from the wrath of God, which is directed at our wickedness, we need more *light* than general revelation affords. General revelation is light to see God, but humans suppress that light. The light of general revelation is utterly insufficient to get back to God. To have real, true, and intimate knowledge of God, we need something else."

"What?" implored Jarrod.

"Special revelation. Where general revelation fails to get us home, special revelation succeeds."

"What is that?" asked Lauren, intrigued.

"The light of special revelation will have to wait until we get out of the darkness of general revelation. I mean this literally," MacGregor said with a chuckle. "It is getting dark out here. Let's collect our things and put them in my car, and then we can go to the bookstore and meet Brad."

Jarrod and Lauren rolled their eyes and groaned, but the growing darkness told them to hurry. The special revelation answer would have to wait.

Chapter 8

Vogue and the Wall Street Journal

AFTER PARKING ON A SIDE STREET, the trio walked along the brick sidewalks, taking in the charm of the old shops. Crowds packed the historic district all summer, but even in the autumn the Strand in downtown Galveston thumped with energy on weekend nights. Tourists took in the scene, availing themselves of the restaurants, bars, and shops that stayed open late for the weekend crowds. The professor steered through the clusters of humanity until they arrived at the Book Nook.

MacGregor knew the store well, but Jarrod and Lauren had never visited it. The name Nook was an understatement. The store took up enormous space, and thousands of books and magazines filled the shelves. They spotted Brad in the magazine section, and Lauren walked up behind him and put her cell phone into his back. "This is a stickup. Your money or your life," she said in her huskiest voice.

"Sorry, sir, I can't help you. I'm an investment banker. There is no distinction between my money and my life."

Lauren laughed and smacked him playfully at the base of his neck. "Now that's a true statement."

Brad turned and saw her and the dress for the first time. As she had hoped, he exhaled. "Wow! You look amazing."

"Thank you, Brad. That's very nice of you." She smiled, partly because she was used to this response, partly because Brad's praise was clearly genuine. "What are you reading?"

Brad held up the latest edition of *Forbes* and indicated an article on a banking merger. "Always looking for valuable information," he said.

"Ah, Bradley Masterson, always focused. Focus brings *success.*" Her sibilant pronunciation emphasized the last word particularly. He couldn't tell whether she was teasing or praising, so he cocked his eyebrows. She cocked hers in mock response, winked, and then whirled, walking down the row of magazines, busying herself in the variety.

Brad watched for a second, but then MacGregor and Jarrod strolled over. MacGregor reached out to shake hands. "Hello, Brad. I'm so glad you could come. You missed a fine picnic dinner, but we're glad you made it to the second half. How was your day?"

Lauren rejoined the group as Brad answered.

"Good to see you, too, Professor. I guess today contained the usual demands, but all in all I'd say it was a good day. And it's great to get out of the office and come down here. It's been awhile since I've been to the beach or anywhere else relaxing. I didn't realize how much I missed it."

Brad turned his attention to his old friend. "Hey, Jarrod." They shook hands while doing the half clasp with their left arms, this being the culturally allowable guy hug, with the requisite slap of each others backs. Two slaps. Friendship and masculinity simultaneously signaled. "How's academia?"

"Great. I've either been in the library or coffee shops in Rice Village all week. Some of the articles are abstruse, but most of the course reading is pretty decent, and I love what I'm learning.

"But right now I couldn't care less. I am just glad to get down here to Galveston and soak up the beach. It was beautiful out there. You missed a great meal."

"OK, OK," Brad protested in mock frustration. "So the deli sandwich and bottled water at the office didn't compare. I don't *even* want to hear about it. Professor MacGregor told me earlier that his wife whipped up quite a feast."

"Yep," said Lauren triumphantly. "And we reveled in a whole lot of sunset and waves, and it was wonderful." She paused a second. "Oh, and the professor turned my views all in a knot, as usual." She flashed her faux-consternation face at MacGregor, who grinned back.

"I'm really sorry I missed *that*," said Brad with enthusiasm. "What did you talk about?"

MacGregor replied serenely, "She already told you, sunset and waves."

"Yeah, right, but what about the Christian stuff? Didn't you continue the theology discussion? Lauren just said you turned her views into a knot. You must have talked about *something* besides creation."

MacGregor, Jarrod, and Lauren exchanged playful smiles and folded their arms. "Nope," said Lauren, "that was about it."

Jarrod intoned with mock gravity, "We worshiped."

"Oh, come on," said Brad. "Why are you being so cagey? What did you talk about?"

Jarrod grimaced. "Neither a poet nor a philosopher are you? Is there any hope for you number-crunching deal makers?" He waited to see what reaction that wrought, and Brad simply raised an eyebrow again, this time in annoyance. "OK, OK. We talked about general revelation."

"OK," Brad responded, obviously in the dark. "And that is . . ." He looked at MacGregor.

"Lauren, why don't you fill Brad in while I get drinks? I'm going to get in line at the in-store coffee shop. Anybody want anything? Jarrod, you're the coffee connoisseur. Do you want to come observe their coffeemaking skills?"

Jarrod laughed. "No, thanks. I'm going to check out some wakeboarding magazines."

MacGregor took drink orders, and after he joined the lengthy line, Lauren began explaining general revelation to Brad. The subject piqued his interest, no doubt, but having Lauren in that sassy dress explain it to him absolutely riveted him. Jarrod glanced over from his place in the magazine rack, and the irritation at Brad and his recent dalliance with Lauren returned mildly, with the added charge of now stealing Lauren's attention.

Eventually they all began to sample the magazines, and Lauren branched off from Brad to look at some of the women's fare. Finally MacGregor hailed them from the coffee shop area. "I've got our drinks and a table. Bring your magazines."

Once they were assembled around the table, MacGregor inquired as to which magazines they had selected.

Jarrod opened up wide the centerfold on his magazine. "Look, it's Parks Bonifay doing a mobius. The dude rocks."

The other three had never heard of Parks Bonifay, less so a mobius, but their eyes told them it must have something to do with the sport of wakeboarding.

"I knew him when I was competing on the wakeboarding circuit. He's the best. He could ride in any kind of water, and in the tournaments he was just ice. Pressure meant nothing to him. I would do great in my practice runs, but when it came to championships, I would choke. Parks never choked. Look at this picture. Is he amazing or what?"

Jarrod couldn't hide his enthusiasm for his friend or the sport. The others had not seen him this excited in a long time.

"Jarrod, I had no idea you were a wakeboarder. You're full of new information tonight, first the travels and now this. When did you compete?" asked MacGregor.

"I rode in high school for three years before going to college. I guess I actually competed for three years. It was a blast. It was something I could do on my own without my parents hassling me."

"How did you do the backpacking if you were competing?" This really interested MacGregor.

"Well, you can't do this forever. It was fun, and I wanted to postpone college, but my parents insisted. They wanted me eventually to get a real job, if you can believe it. So we argued a lot, but then they threatened to pull the plug on me, and since my SAT score got me into UT Plan II, I guess the threat helped move me along."

He slid down in the chair, sticking his legs out away from the table, and scanned the bookstore in his carefree manner. Lauren and Brad knew the story, but the details were fuzzy since they hadn't talked about this for so long.

"OK, to be honest, I just wasn't good enough. I had a few sponsors, and I was somewhere in the top twenty, but I couldn't crack the top ten. I could ride with the top dudes really well when we were just having fun, but too often I would miss my big stunts in the championship runs. I got pretty frustrated. I still ride when I can for fun, but to compete takes four or five hours of practice a day, every day, to pull off the stunts."

Lauren always loved hearing about Jarrod's extreme-sport existence. She loved to water-ski, and the families of several of her sorority sisters had lake houses and speedboats on Lake Travis and Lake McQueeney. Lauren and her sisters escaped to McQueeney many times during college. Brad, though impressed that Jarrod had attained top-twenty status, viewed wakeboarders as he did surfers: fun lives, good athletes, but irresponsible people who were dodging real life. As much as Brad loved thrill-seeking adventures, he never understood how Jarrod could seriously contemplate blowing off college for the sport.

MacGregor, however, recognized real life when he saw it. He saw Jarrod's zeal and obvious happiness. And more importantly, he wanted to understand why Jarrod left behind this source of joy.

"Who decides who wins championships?"

"A panel of judges. They assess your stunts for technical execution, style—stuff like that."

"How do they get to be judges?"

"I don't know. Some used to be riders. I really don't know. There's a lot of politics."

"And how did they determine the top-twenty rankings?"

"Performance in tournaments."

"Interesting. Does this magazine have a lot of say about who's in and who's out in terms of being good in your sport?"

"Well, yeah. This is kind of *it.* I mean, all the sponsors have ads in here, and they always have articles about new moves and behind-the-scenes stuff. Interviews. Of course all the pictures. So yeah, this is kind of the official scene. We all read it."

"Brad, Lauren, did you two know about this world of wakeboarding?"

Brad shook his head. "Only what Jarrod used to say about it."

Lauren replied, "I've heard of it even apart from Jarrod. I've seen wakeboarders when I've been out water-skiing. But I've never noticed the magazine before."

Jarrod shrugged his shoulders, unperturbed. "That's all right. It's my private world. Some of the best times I have are riding. I love it."

"Jarrod, your world fascinates me. I'd love to go with you someday when you do it again. I've driven many a boat in my time. If you don't mind letting me drive, you could show me your moves," said MacGregor.

"Sure. That would be great. We'll do it."

"Jarrod, Brad says he doesn't really know about your world. Which makes me wonder, do you know about *his* world? Brad, what magazines were you looking at?"

Brad pushed his magazines away from their stacked position so that their covers could be seen. "*Golf Digest* and *Forbes.*"

MacGregor reached out for *Golf Digest.* "Oh yes, I've read this a few times. Just enough to mess up my swing."

Brad laughed with him. "You got it. I'm starting to learn that if I do everything their experts suggest, I will eventually be a disaster. Sometimes their instructions seem to just flat-out contradict the articles from previous issues. But I still like reading it. It's fun to keep up with equipment and different courses."

"Jarrod, Lauren, do either of you play golf?"

Lauren answered first. "No, but I want to learn. It's something I should pick up. As my career progresses, the work will center more on relationships with clients, and golf is a great way to develop those relationships. All the men associates play when they can, and some of the women are picking it up."

Jarrod shook his head. "I've played before, but I never got into it. It's kind of why I got into wakeboarding; golf was my parents' thing. All their friends play a lot and travel around to different resorts to play. Of course, I never had the attention span for golf, so I was never good enough, and it just made my dad mad. It was embarrassing to him. So, I said, 'Forget this,' and got into wakeboarding."

MacGregor fingered the *Golf Digest* magazine and asked, "Have you all read this?"

Both Lauren and Jarrod shook their heads.

"Play a game with me, kind of a thought experiment. If I offered to pay you each $100 to tell me about the world of golf—including personalities, courses, tournaments, swing advice, equipment advice— where would you go?"

Jarrod said, "The Internet has everything. Google is *magic*. I could probably find everything you need that way. But I might also go talk to an old pro at a country club. Or I might read a book by Tiger Woods— if he's written one—or (looking down at the magazine on the table) I guess I'd read a bunch of these magazines."

Lauren concurred. "Yes, I'd probably talk to some golfers I know at the firm and check the Internet, but I'd read this magazine too."

Brad's brow furrowed. "Why did you ask that, Professor? Help me out here with your thought experiment. Why would you care if they know about golf? Who would pay somebody a lot of money to learn that kind of stuff?"

"Brad, I know it's a silly question. I'm just trying to understand how each of you thinks. I could ask the same questions about understanding the business world, and you'd probably say successful businesspeople, professors at your business school, this *Forbes* magazine you've got here. Also, you probably subscribe to the *Wall Street Journal.* Maybe watch Bloomberg's on TV. Right?"

"Sure," Brad said. "I get information from all those sources and dozens more. Information is the coin of the realm in my business."

"Can you think of an enterprise in which information is *not* the coin of the realm?" asked MacGregor.

Brad pondered that for a moment. Certainly all his work as an associate at the bank centered on accessing, manipulating, and packaging information. The energy companies he worked with on deals depended on information. His lawyer friends depended on information. Two buddies from UT days toiled in residency programs, and they were constantly seeking as much medical information as they could from colleagues, medical journals, and the like. His friends in consulting, yes. The venture capital guys, yes.

"I guess you're right. I guess I'm so in the groove of my own work that I don't usually think about these other jobs. But, yeah, everybody does need information to succeed."

"Lauren?"

"Same for attorneys. I spend all day trafficking in information, much of it the same information Brad and his associates are dealing with. And 'go-bys'—at my level as a third-year associate, I'm always questing for the perfect 'go-by' to help me draft the next document. Information is critical to practicing law."

"I'm sure. But I bet you didn't pick up magazines about the law tonight. Did you also get financial magazines?"

"Nope. This is like a mini-vacation. Above Average Brad can't get away from it, but I can, so no, I didn't scoop up a bunch of work-related stuff."

"Which magazines did you get?" inquired MacGregor.

"Guess. If I didn't get business 'zines, what do you think I got?"

MacGregor looked at her and thought for a moment. "Well, you dress very fashionably. My guess is that you got women's fashion magazines."

Lauren pursed her lips and nodded. "Nice guess, Sherlock. *Elle* caught my eye before coming over here." Her arms had been resting on the table, obscuring the magazine, but as she now leaned back in her chair, she revealed the *Elle.*

"Do you read other magazines like it?" the professor inquired.

"Sure. My girlfriends and I read *Vogue,* things like that."

"What attracts you to those?"

"The fashion, for one. They're all different. They have different target audiences. But the articles are hip about what's going on, relationships, how to handle workplace situations. Some of it is pretty hokey, but there's a lot of helpful information as well."

"Brad, Jarrod, ever read these?"

"No," came the emphatic stereo reply.

"We've all got our own worlds," said MacGregor. "I actually read a lot of academic journals of theology and biblical studies, but they don't carry such material here. But I might have picked up *Christianity Today* or *Christian Century,* and this place even carries *Regeneration Quarterly.* You've probably never heard of *Christianity Today* magazine or *RQ* have you?"

The others admitted they hadn't.

"You see, we've all got our own worlds. And we each know where to go for information. I think we agree that information is the coin of the realm for all endeavors, so you need to know where to go. But why do you go to *specific* sources for information?"

"They're the ones that have it," answered Brad. "Like the *Journal,* they've got information I need for daily context and news in the financial markets."

"But how do you know the *Journal* has correct information or that they have selected the right stories, writers, and articles to publish?"

Brad had never even thought of that before. "I just do. It's the *Journal.* Everybody reads the *Journal.*"

"So if you read it in the *Journal,* you're confident of its merit and accuracy."

"Yes. It may not be absolutely perfect in every article, but yeah, I trust what I read there."

"Do you realize, Brad, that you let writers determine your information flow? Or high-level sources with an agenda that choose to leak information to a *Journal* writer. More precisely, a managing editor determines what you think is the right take on the issues he or she deems most important. That's remarkable control over your information source and thus over your thinking. If the *Journal* shapes your coin of the realm, then it shapes a lot of what you think, say, or do in a day."

"But that's taking this way too far. I do my own thinking. My team and I hash out issues before making big decisions. Besides, I've worked hard for a great education, and all that I've learned in college and business school comes to bear on my thinking each day. The *Journal* doesn't *shape* my thinking."

"Brad, all that is true, and you've already mentioned that you have dozens of other information sources besides the *Journal.* I'm just using the *Journal* as a case in point. But the *Journal* is one of the most prominent in your daily intake of information, yes? Think about it—the editor controls part of what you read or don't read just by his decision to select material and writers. Then the perspective of each writer, who has his or her own biases, gives you that specific window into an event or issue. You don't get *all* camera angles, if you will. You get one. And that means your information is limited by *selection* and *perspective.* This doesn't mean you are a robot; it just means that all your education and your nimble mind have only material to work with that the *Journal* editor packages for you."

"OK, sure. I see that. I've just never considered this in terms of the selection and packaging of my information before."

MacGregor moved on to Lauren. "Lauren, is what you're wearing tonight fashionable?"

Startled, as if MacGregor had asked an impertinent question, she replied, "Of course. I keep up with current styles."

"How would you back up your contention that your dress is fashionable? I look around this coffee shop area, and I can also see around the bookstore, and few women are wearing anything similar to your dress. Based on the folks around us, it would seem that your dress is not fashionable."

"Yes, but you can't use them. They aren't into fashion. Look, it's mostly just casual clothes tonight because we're at the beach. And those jeans and that top on that girl are fine but not really trendy. Well, that top is somewhat trendy, but pairing it with jeans just doesn't make the mark." Waving her hand in a circle, she said, "These other folks are dressed fine, but you can tell they didn't buy their clothes this season."

"So how can you persuade me that what you're wearing is 'in'?"

"It just *is.* I *know* fashion. I keep up with it. It's important to me to look my best." This whole conversation struck her as funny.

"There's no way to prove it?"

"I could show you fashion shows on TV or have you meet with a fashion critic."

"How about the magazine in your hand?"

"Well, sure, but not for this dress. This is early autumn wear, and this issue of *Elle* has spreads on the new winter lines. But you could go back and look at a spring issue and you'd see dresses like this one all over the place. Of course, they don't look nearly as good on those tall girls in the magazines," Lauren joked.

"And this is where you get your information about fashion. If information is the coin of the realm and your endeavor is to be dressed fashionably, you can go to *Vogue* or *Elle,* and you'll get the information you need."

"Sure. There are other sources as well, but in terms of normal everyday life, these are the most prominent ones."

MacGregor paused and looked around at each of them. "We each have little subcultures or worlds. Some are work related, others are hobbies, and others are matters of dress. Each world has its information, and if you are to succeed in a particular world and really know the ins and outs of the world, you need to go to a good source for your information. So you need to go to the right authorities—*Wakeboard Magazine, Golf Digest,* the *Wall Street Journal, Elle*—to be sure you have the right information."

Jarrod shrugged his shoulders. Why was MacGregor belaboring the point? Brad's eyes narrowed. He could see the wily professor "setting the table," but he couldn't yet discern the goal. Lauren nodded knowingly. Her communication training harmonized with what MacGregor said. Clients had to trust her as an authority before they would accept her legal advice. If clients had other authorities, like aggressive bankers pitching a deal, inclining them away from her and her partners' legal opinions, then she had to undermine the client's trust in those competing authorities.

"What's the point? Where are you going with all of this information and authority business?" Jarrod wanted MacGregor to show his cards.

MacGregor considered Jarrod's question and then addressed Brad. "Brad, did Lauren tell you about the doctrine of general revelation?"

"Yes. I had never thought of it quite that way before, but I definitely believe that God reveals himself through creation. I have never explored the idea of people being made with the sense of the divine and the moral law on our hearts, but it makes sense. Lauren said you discussed the problem of how God reveals himself generally, but people suppress the truth by their wickedness and thus earn God's wrath. She said you said that general revelation gave the whole world 'light' about God, but since people reject it to go their own way, they are judged."

"Very nice. Well done, Lauren," complimented the professor.

"Thank you," said Lauren, as she imitated the motion of a curtsy. "I have a great teacher."

"Brad, you've articulated the problem. The world has knowledge of God through creation, but the world spurns the Lord and worships created things instead. Furthermore, people violate the conscience that God has embedded in their hearts, resulting in opposition to his holy precepts. And, as you said, the result is wrath and judgment.

"Now Lauren and Jarrod think this is a problem because the information pouring forth through creation doesn't leave people in a good place. It leaves them in a bad place—judgment. However, they are without excuse. Lauren and Jarrod want to know how to get people who have access to all this general revelation out of trouble. The information that God reveals about himself in general revelation is not enough. I told them what is needed is special revelation."

"OK. But I don't know what special revelation is either. I've never even heard the phrase before." All three, knowing resolution awaited, looked intently at the professor.

"The connection is this: if general revelation contains lots of information, but that information is not enough to get you right with God, what information do you need? You need special revelation. Remember, each of us has our own worlds, and in each world information is the coin of the realm. We each know which authorities to go to for the right information in our worlds. Likewise, in God's world, ultimate reality, information is still the coin of the realm. The big question is, where do we go to get the right information for getting accepted by God? Or, to put it another way, what authority do we trust to tell us the information about being acceptable to God?"

He continued. "Not just *anyone's* opinion will do for getting the bead on fashion or about financial matters or who the really good wakeboarders are. It is possible to get wrong information from inadequate or illegitimate authorities. So if we want to get good information from the right authority about getting right with God, where do we go?"

Brad replied, "The Bible."

Jarrod jumped in, "The Bible's fine. But you could also just go to the Holy Spirit. Or worship. My church is all about getting people right with God. It happens to me every week during praise and worship. I'm concerned about you overemphasizing the Bible and not emphasizing the Spirit. I'm telling you, the Holy Spirit is powerful; the Spirit tells us what we need to know in relation to God. I see it happen all the time, and we don't spend much time on the Bible. Everyone just gets jacked about the Spirit."

Brad remembered his visits to Spirit's Power Fellowship with Jarrod. Jarrod's pastors, who alternated the preaching responsibility, used the Bible in a well-meaning way. However, their lack of training and their emphasis on individuals' getting a "direct word from the Spirit" meant the Bible functioned as something of a magical book of quotes, which were serviceable for the topic of the day. Brad disdained this approach to God's Word, but Lauren disdained the Bible itself.

Lauren looked at Jarrod, clearly weirded out. She thought, *What on earth does he mean, 'jacked about the Spirit'? Sometimes he can be so bizarre.* "Well, Jarrod, you *know* this is definitely out of my comfort zone. But, Professor, I've also told you a few times that I think the Bible is full of fairy tales and contradictions. There may be some good stories, but that's no different from other peoples' sacred books. In fact, it's no different from any good literature."

Brad winced. "Lauren, I can prove it to you. If you're open-minded and objective, you will see that the Bible is the Word of God. But you are so biased that you'll probably never see it. If you were neutral and looked at all the evidence in an unbiased way, you'd see that the Bible is God's Word."

Lauren, aghast, reacted. "*Me* biased? *Me?* Are you kidding me, Brad Masterson? You're the one who believes this fruit-loop superstition while the rest of the world has moved on. A thousand years ago, fine, but now science and spirituality have progressed, and we don't need fairy tales. Do you not realize that *normal* people aren't Christians? Do you not realize that the normal world makes fun of you people because you believe such bizarre things? Get real! The fact that you believe in a book this old to tell you about what's true and right is either pathetic or scary. So don't be telling *me* about being biased. It's you Christians who are not objective."

Needless to say, the effect of such an acrimonious speech, delivered passionately and loudly, was to embarrass the rest of them. People at other tables in the Book Nook coffee shop looked at them, as did people in line to order. Lauren realized she had been too loud and instantly regretted it, but Brad had gotten her goat, and she was angry.

MacGregor endured the barrage, but, as on several previous occasions, he intervened with directness. "OK, gang, let's de-escalate. Come on."

"Well, she started it," said Jarrod in a mock child's whine, a huge grin on his face. "Make her go sit in the corner."

"Let's all go to a corner like they do in boxing," suggested MacGregor. "This worked well the last time we got tense at Common Grounds. I need to use the rest room myself. Let's take a couple minutes for a recess."

Lauren and Brad didn't even make eye contact as they rose from the table. Jarrod slugged them both in the arm and said, "Chill, guys. The professor's right."

Lauren's face betrayed no sign of giving an inch. She turned on her heel and followed MacGregor to the rest room area. "You've stirred up the hornet's nest," Jarrod remarked to Brad.

Brad gave Jarrod a baleful look. "This time she stirred it up. I've got her on this one. I've got evidence."

Jarrod reached Brad's shoulder and squeezed. "Come on, amigo. Let's go check out the desserts."

Chapter 9

Stories We Live By

MACGREGOR'S TACTICAL INTERRUPTION alleviated things a bit, but when they all reconvened, Lauren still had her jaw set, and Brad still itched to close the deal on Lauren's flawed thinking.

"I agree with Professor MacGregor," Brad said. "Let's keep the personal attacks out of it. Let's keep it *all* objective and talk about the evidence. Professor, if your question is, What is the authority that tells us how to get right with God? we need to give Lauren the evidence for why Scripture is the Word of God."

Lauren, cheeks still flushed with indignation, looked at MacGregor. His eyes sparkled and he exuded so much relaxed confidence, looking directly at her, that her face softened, and the barest hint of a smile creased her lips. She wanted to engage Brad's new salvo, but she caught MacGregor's eye, and she felt surprised that her desire to please MacGregor outstripped her desire to pummel Brad. OK, she would de-escalate, even if Brad wouldn't.

"Professor, I'm sorry. I shouldn't have said those things about Christians. I didn't mean you, just the extremist wackos we hear about. But I shouldn't have said all that."

"Thank you, Lauren. Apology accepted. And besides, you're at least half right."

This announcement snapped Jarrod and Brad's heads up in surprise.

"What?" Brad exclaimed. He expected the seminary professor with years of accumulated knowledge to eviscerate Lauren, not endorse her.

Lauren was just as surprised but equal to the moment. "Of course I'm half right," she said with a wink, "but undoubtedly I'm right on the other half as well."

"Brad," MacGregor stated, "she's right about us Christians being biased. We're not objective."

"What? Professor, we're talking about the Bible. Come on. You know the evidence. I *know* you know all this."

"Oh, Brad, I assure you I do. I used all those arguments for years. They were more persuasive to people back in the 1960s and '70s but less so now.

"I still personally accept those evidences, and by that I mean that they make sense to me. They're not *wrong* to bring up. If you've used these evidences in the past with your peers, Brad, surely you've seen how ineffective they are these days. But effectiveness is not really the point. What I'm really saying is that I am not objective and neither are you."

"See," said Lauren, "normal people are the objective ones."

"Then normal people don't exist," said the professor dryly.

"What? You just said that *Christians* are biased," said Lauren.

"We are, but so is everyone else. Everyone is biased. No one is neutral. All of us have precommitments. I've yet to meet someone who transcends his or her social location."

"Social location?" queried Jarrod.

"A person's family background, social class, education, race, the kind of subcultures the person grew up in."

"What does that have to do with evidence and rational thought and debating what is true?" asked Jarrod. "In all the philosophy work I've done, I don't think we've spent ten minutes talking about a philosopher's social status. I mean, analytic philosophy is the pursuit of truth, the history of ideas. It's a rational pursuit."

"Well, actually, many philosophers have developed sensitivity to how cultural contexts affect what people believe. Certainly theologians pay increasing, if sometimes grudging, attention to social location and its effect on knowledge. As for philosophers who don't consider this, I don't know what to say. At this point in academia, it's pretty hard to ignore the effects of social location on peoples' thinking.

"But back to what I was saying to Lauren. We are all influenced by our social location. We all have presuppositions that govern the rest of our thinking. If you conceive of all that you believe as a web of ideas, the presuppositions would be those key ideas at the core of the web."

"But, Professor, what about scientists? They're objective. They just deal with facts," Lauren proffered.

MacGregor laughed. "Oh, no. Scientists have their presuppositions too. If we use that web metaphor, scientists also have beliefs at the core of their webs that are their primary beliefs. For example, science presupposes that nature is all there is. Scientists observe nature, and they presume that everything can be explained by natural causes. *By definition* they exclude supernatural factors. When God, who is *supernatural*, interacts with nature, scientists can't even address it since they have already excluded any supernatural factors."

"But they're still objective," countered Lauren.

"Well, actually, they're not. Their worldview has its own assumptions, rules, conventions, and methodology. *Within* that realm they play by their rules, and they do fine. But they cannot deal with things that fall *outside* their realm."

"But they deal with facts. Everyone knows that scientists deal with facts."

"Lauren, there is no such thing as a brute fact. All so-called facts are viewed by a subject, a person looking at the facts. What person is totally objective? When a person observes a fact, he or she sees it through a lens. We all have lenses."

"What do you mean by *lens?*" asked Lauren.

"Each person has a worldview or a set of lenses through which he or she looks at the world. You can compare these mental lenses to sunglasses. For example, why do you personally wear sunglasses?"

"To look cool," Lauren replied, deadpan. "But seriously, to keep light out of my eyes."

"And what kind of lenses do you buy when you shop for sunglasses? I'm not talking frames but the actual lenses. Is there anything you look for in particular?"

"Yeah, they need to have UV protection."

"Why?"

"Because UV rays are bad for your eyes and your skin."

"So when sunlight strikes your lenses, what happens to the harmful UV rays?"

"They're blocked," said Lauren with a shrug.

"Exactly," said MacGregor. "The lenses filter out the UV rays, but they let other rays in. You're not in the dark; you're not left without *any* sunlight, just without the UV rays that are part of the sun's light waves."

"OK, what's your point?"

"I'm getting there," he said warmly, "but I want to add to this illustration. Sunglasses with UV protection serve one function. How about rose-colored glasses?"

Now that Jarrod lived in the grad student culture, sometimes he wore his old rad wakeboarding attire. He weighed in as the resident authority since he donned a dizzying array of killer shades. "They make everything red. It's pretty cool."

Brad added, "Yes, that old expression about someone looking at the world through rose-colored glasses. It's a metaphor for someone who turns a blind eye to negative things and sees or remembers only the good."

Lauren couldn't resist. "Really, Brad? Is that where that comes from?"

MacGregor skipped over her sarcasm. "Do you see? The *normal* sunglasses filter out UV rays, but rose-colored glasses filter out rays in the color spectrum of the light wave so that everything looks reddish. It all depends on what the lens is made of. The same light strikes all the lenses, but some lenses are made of material that filters out one part of the light wave, and different lenses filter out other parts of the light wave.

"What's my point? Objects are not seen exactly *as they are,* but rather they are seen as they pass *through* our lenses. Depending on the lens, the same object will appear different to different people."

"It makes sense. I haven't heard anyone put it this way before, but it definitely relates to the idea of people having their own opinions on things. I assume that lenses are made by our experiences," said Lauren.

"That's right," replied MacGregor. "Family is probably the strongest factor in constructing an individual's lens. Also things like pop culture around you in the form of movies, TV, music, fashion. Of course, language, religious beliefs, and socioeconomic status are enormously important factors in shaping our lenses."

"So everyone's lenses are different."

"Exactly," said the professor. "That's precisely my point. *Everybody* has different lenses, so no one looks at an object the same way. We may see things similarly to some people, differently than others."

"OK, I agree with all that. But I'm not sure about the point you are trying to make," said Lauren, a little on edge.

"My point is that there are no brute facts. Every object or every fact is interpreted through a lens. Scientists have lenses just like anyone else. Their lenses get shaped in school, by teachers, by professors at the university, by science books and science journals, and more."

"Isn't that good?" asked Lauren. "Isn't that what gives them the knowledge to be good at what they do?"

"Sure," replied MacGregor, "and I have great respect for the rigorous education they receive in order to develop finely tuned lenses. Being steeped in the rules, assumptions, and methods of science has enabled scientists to do wonders in helping us understand the world around us.

But they are not objective. Social forces, conditioning, politics, and culture affect scientists just as they affect nonscientists. Everything that they see and that we see is interpreted."

"OK, I can see that we interpret everything, but don't you think their conclusions are right? I mean, most people acknowledge scientists are on the right track."

"Hmm, this is going to be more complicated to answer. To talk about a person's worldview, we can use a number of metaphors. I've already mentioned a web as one metaphor and lenses as another. When you ask, 'Are the conclusions of a scientist right?' you can't help but deal with their worldview or web or lens. Each web or lens has these presuppositions. These are beliefs that are assumed, and they are the 'first belief,' if you will, of a person. Not first in time but first in priority. Everything a person believes in his or her web of beliefs stems from those primary beliefs at the center of the web. Or, to use the lens metaphor, the presuppositions are the key materials that compose the lens and thus govern what information passes through.

"And here's another thing: these presuppositions *determine* the ultimate conclusions. Or, to come at it from the other direction, the conclusions have something of the presuppositions embedded in them."

Brad broke in, "Professor, I understand your criticizing science this way, but you're not distinguishing Christianity and the Bible from science. You're making it sound like Christians are the same way with our conclusions."

"Yes, I am."

"How can you say that?" Brad asked incredulously. "You're a Christian! Don't you realize what you're saying?"

"Maybe not. What do you hear me saying?"

"All this stuff about presuppositions determining conclusions and conclusions having presuppositions embedded in them, don't you realize how circular that is?"

"Brad, of course I do. In a sense our beliefs are circular."

"But that means they're wrong. That means you think Christianity is illogical!" Brad exclaimed.

Jarrod spoke up, "Actually not. While I haven't thought about the social location idea, I do remember Dr. Leider lecturing on how philosophical systems are all interconnected."

"Connected, fine. But what the professor is talking about is circular reasoning."

"I don't know, Brad. The assumptions of any philosophy entail its conclusions. It's actually bad logic if the conclusion is not tied to the assumptions."

"But all my life I've heard that circular reasoning is wrong. You can't just say, 'Such and such is true because such and such is true.' You can't say blue is better than red because blue is better than red."

"Brad, you're right," responded the professor. "I hope I'm not suggesting anything like the example you just gave. However, if I give evidences for any contention in a debate, the opposing debater will push and push and ask why, why, why until we get back to my presuppositions. What is persuasive or satisfactory evidence to me is evidence that meets the standards of my worldview. My worldview supplies the standards for the evidences that persuade it. Thus you can see that in an ultimate sense, there *is* some circularity there. And this is true for any worldview, any system."

"I'm sorry, Professor. You know I respect you, but this just goes against everything I've ever heard. I'm going to have to respectfully disagree."

MacGregor chuckled. "That's quite all right, Brad. I've never thought another person would agree with everything I say. And I understand your position. For many years I believed that way and taught that way. It wasn't easy for me to change my perspective on these things."

"What happened?" asked Jarrod. "Why did you change?"

"It's an interesting thing. Three things converged in my life, and over time I began to reevaluate how I understood the Scriptures. I'd love to tell you the whole story, but that's just going to have to be one more thing we set aside for a later discussion. Otherwise we'll get entirely away from our conversation. But one of those three factors is important for today's topic, and that's the concept of story."

Brad remained wary, but Jarrod and Lauren found this intriguing. "What do you mean by 'the concept of story'?" she asked.

"A few decades ago, intellectuals in Europe and the United States began to talk about worldviews as stories or narratives. Remember that a few minutes ago I used two metaphors for worldviews: a web of beliefs and a set of lenses. There is a third metaphor we can use for worldviews, and it's actually my favorite. This is the concept of story. You can see a worldview as a large story that gives information about the world and supplies meaning for life.

"This was one of the three factors that converged for me and opened my eyes to new ways of understanding Scripture. I became aware of academic leaders talking about science as a story, Christianity as a story, economics as a story. Basically every worldview, every religion, and even a secular system like science is a narrative."

"Do you mean philosophies are stories too?" asked Jarrod.

"Yes, that's good, Jarrod. Each philosophical camp is a story too. Forgive me, but you know my love for memorizing quotes. Trevor Hart, in his book *Faith Thinking,* wrote, 'Every human community has a story which it tells both to itself and others concerning its distinctive origins and *raison d'etre,* and about the sort of place this world in which it exists is.'"

"What does that mean?" asked Brad.

"Well, *raison d'etre* is a French phrase for 'reason for existence.' Hart says that every community has stories by which it explains origins, the nature of humanity, destiny, morality. Stories shape and provide boundaries for a community, and thus stories create the identity of the community and the individuals that comprise it."

Brad persisted, "How does this relate to Christianity's being objective truth?"

"I was trying to explain how I changed my mind from thinking all the evidences could compel someone to accept the Bible as authoritative. Lauren, if you'll remember, said she thought the Bible was rife with fairy tales and contradictions. And you wanted to detail a number of evidences that you think will persuade her to believe in the Bible. I used to think that way—about deploying evidences for the reliability of the Scriptures—but I learned through experience that this simply doesn't persuade many people today.

"But more importantly, I began to learn why. Now I realize that we inhabit communities of stories. These stories, again, are like webs or lenses. The stories govern how we think about ourselves and others. They shape our interpretation of everything. Since we live by scripts supplied to us by the culture that surrounds us, we are not interpreting information objectively. Of course, God *is* objective, absolute truth, but no human is.

"People see things according to their community's story. Lauren has a worldview, or a story, by which she understands life. She lives in a community that has a story. Again, by *story* I mean ideas about the origin of the world, what humans are like, what is moral, and human destiny. But Lauren's story is in many ways antithetical to the Christian story, and when the worldviews or stories collide, the people who inhabit Lauren's story shrewdly seek to undermine the Scriptures."

"That's why we give them that book of evidences for Christianity being true," replied Brad.

"Brad, there's nothing wrong with giving a skeptic that book. Many people have been helped by that book. It's particularly reassuring to Christians who have doubts. But is it effective with people today who are outside the faith? And a more critical question is, should we *expect* it to be effective? Think about it: since the Bible is the bedrock of the

Christian story, the so-called evidences for the Scriptures' reliability make sense to us. The evidences fit our story, which is already rooted in Scripture. But those evidences often just bounce off people like Lauren who are *committed* to opposing beliefs. These evidences are not compelling to people like her because they have a different understanding of the world. And, if I try to recast Christianity to conform to their stories and standards of truth, I will dishonor God and be guilty of watering down the Christian faith."

"But if she would just be open-minded, she could look at the evidences neutrally, and those evidences would prove the Bible is true. Thus our story is true," said Brad.

MacGregor's lips pressed into a tight, thin-lipped smile. He sat back in his chair and looked at his hands on the table in a distant, preoccupied way. He audibly exhaled and finally looked back at Brad. "Brad, the irony is that you're hearing me give reasons for my view, and it's bouncing off of you. Our exchange is a microcosm of what I'm trying to say. You are committed to your story. In this case, to extend the story metaphor, you're committed to a substory or a story within the larger story. You are committed to the idea of objectivity, to neutrality. You believe that there are facts out there just waiting to be discovered or observed.

"I doubt this will be persuasive to you, but I'll try to express again what I did a couple of minutes ago. There is no neutrality. We're all committed to deeply held presuppositions. Anyone who thinks he is neutral is blind to his own precommitments, or he is intentionally masquerading as unbiased so that he can overpower another's arguments."

"I just can't see this," said Brad in response. "This sounds so loosey-goosey. I like cold, hard facts."

"So do I," Lauren chimed in.

"Fine," replied MacGregor, with a resigned shrug. "Do it your way. Have your big debate. Argue your points. Get frustrated with each other. Go home to your separate groups of friends and recount the whole conversation and watch your friends nod and join you in mocking the other's inability to reason. Go ahead and marvel at how *blind* the other person is. And you'll be acting out what I'm telling you."

"Which is? . . ." Brad asked with an arched tone.

"That Lauren inhabits a community that has lenses or a story that understands reality differently than your community does. You have your lens or story, and Lauren has hers, and the arguments and points from each other will be unpersuasive because it won't fit your community's stories."

"What are we supposed to do?" asked Jarrod. "I thought you were making the case that we need an authority that gives us information about getting right with God. All of that about information being the coin of the realm. How does the concept of story fit in?"

"Christianity is a story. Because this appears to be a new concept to you all, I'll say it again. Christianity is a story of our *origins*—how and why God made us, and our *natures*—what we're like, and our *destiny*—where we're going. I remember in church camp one summer in high school when the whole story was explained by the speaker during the evening services. For three days I peppered him with questions during lunch about what he had said the night before. As I think about him now, I'm sure he had never heard of intellectuals talking about worldviews and stories, and besides, it was years before academics started talking about narratives. But he knew the Scriptures as a story. He explained how God made us for himself, but we chased after sin, and how ever since God has chased after us. He sent Jesus to find us and bring us home. It's a wonderful story, and when I heard it, God touched my heart, and I believed."

"That's how you became a Christian?" asked Jarrod.

"Yes. Granted, there was a whole lot more detail, and the speaker took us on a whole tour of the Bible from Genesis to Revelation to unfold the story to us. As the speaker was explaining the Scriptures, God illumined my heart and mind, and suddenly it all made sense."

"That's really cool." Jarrod loved hearing stories about the personal, real dimension of Christian living. "I want to hear more about your life and how you came to believe all the things you do. But I'm still not seeing how this relates to general revelation and information being the coin of the realm," said Jarrod.

"OK, back to the original question. Information is crucial for making right decisions, and we know from Romans 1 that God has revealed himself through general revelation. However, people suppress the knowledge of God, and consequently God has wrath toward people who worship idols instead of himself, the Creator God. General revelation isn't enough to change our hearts and minds so that we can have knowledge of God. That's a problem. Where do we go to get accurate, true information about how to become acceptable to God? His Word. Just as the *Wall Street Journal* or *Golf Digest* or *Elle* or *Wakeboarding* are the key authorities in your worlds, the Bible is the authority on how to get right with God."

"And of course I disagree with what you're saying because we have different lenses. So you can't prove that the Bible is the authority on how to be accepted by God," said Lauren.

"You're right; I can't prove it to someone who is committed to his or her autonomous standards of truth. I can't persuade someone who is committed to another system or story. And they can't *prove* their systems to me."

"I do see this. It's just another way of saying everyone sees things his or her own way. It's strange how I believed everyone has his or her own views, and yet I've also totally believed that there are facts that everyone can see."

"That's pretty common, Lauren. Many of my seminary students over the years have had just such an eclectic group of conflicting beliefs. Part of my task is to help students recognize their beliefs and untangle some of the conflicts."

Brad realized that Jarrod and Lauren were tracking with MacGregor's ideas about lenses and stories, and that awareness created a sense of being left behind in the conversation. But he was suspicious of MacGregor's perspective. It sounded liberal to him, or at least on the slippery slope to liberalism, and ever since undergrad days at UT, he'd felt resentment at theological liberals who tried to undermine historic Christianity. It wasn't that he couldn't learn new things about the faith but rather that he was cautious—very cautious—about embracing new views on Scripture. But his native curiosity and desire not to be left behind in the conversation prompted him to ask a question.

"You keep using the word *presupposition.* You said something earlier about presuppositions being ideas that govern our other beliefs. This seems to be the bottom line of what you're saying, so maybe if I understand this . . ."

"Great. Look, Brad, I understand this is new. When I began to encounter this perspective years ago, I thought it was dangerous and a threat to orthodox Christianity. But what I came to see is that my view about objectivity and neutrality did not come from the Scriptures, and it did not come from the church in most of her history. No, the ideas about objectivity and neutrality came from the Enlightenment philosophers and became ingrained in European and American Christianity.

"To answer your question, presuppositions are precommitments. Everybody has to start thinking somewhere. My favorite theologian, Augustine, said *'Credo ut intelligam.'* In English that means, 'I believe in order that I may know.' We all have beliefs we presuppose or believe at the outset, and we go from there. And like I said earlier, I'm not neutral. I'm not unbiased. I'm not objective, but no one is. We are all committed.

"What am I committed to? My commitment is to the Lord and his Word. Another great Christian thinker, C. S. Lewis, said it best: 'I believe in Christianity as I believe that the sun has risen, not only because I see it, but because by it I see everything else.' I see everything in light of Christ and his Word. That's part of what it means for me to submit to Jesus as my Lord in all things, including how I think."

"That sounds a little better to me," said Brad, still wary but slightly assuaged, "and I'm definitely relieved to hear you say you believe in the Bible all the way. I still don't get the metaphor of the story and how everything lives in a community of a story, but oh well. Maybe that's because I deal in the world of finance."

"Oh, that's a story in itself, too, but I'm not going to belabor the point, Brad. If you dislike it or disagree, that's fine."

"But I do want to hear why you think the Bible is true from within Christianity. Even if you won't give Lauren all the outside, objective proofs for the Bible, can't you tell her what the evidence book calls internal evidence?"

"Yes, I can. That's an excellent suggestion, and I suspect it would be useful for Jarrod, as well." Jarrod nodded. "Lauren, do you mind? I realize showing you these verses might not persuade you that the Bible is the Word of God, but wouldn't you like to see for yourself what the Bible says about itself?"

"I guess," Lauren said drolly. "It can't hurt."

"Excellent. Brad, did you want to show these verses yourself?"

"Sure. I'm a bit rusty. I haven't gone through a list of verses about what the Bible claims about itself in several years. But I did this so much in college in my campus fellowship that I think it'll all come back. I know for starters we need to go to 2 Timothy 3:16. Professor, do you have your Bible?"

MacGregor produced his slender Bible, and Brad began hunting down the verse.

"Here it is. 'All Scripture is God-breathed and is useful for teaching, rebuking, correcting and training in righteousness.' You see, the Bible not only says that it is useful for teaching, and so on, but most importantly it is God-breathed."

"I can tell that it means it's God's Word, but that just sounds kind of funny. Why 'inspired'?" inquired Lauren.

Brad had used this verse in debates with others so many times that he simply took for granted that 'inspired' simply meant the Bible was God's Word. He had never actually paused to reflect on what 'inspired by God' actually meant or how it functioned in Scripture's origin.

MacGregor observed Brad trying to answer and came to the rescue. "Lauren, as usual, you ask a revealing question. Have you heard of the Holy Spirit, say when a priest or minister says he is baptizing a person in the name of the Father, the Son, and the Holy Spirit?"

Lauren thought back for a moment to religious services she'd been invited to for friends and family and recalled the phrase. "Yes, I think so."

"The Greek word for *spirit* is *pneuma,* which relates to breath and wind. And if you know about the English word *inspire,* you know that it has to do with breath. Someone who is inspired is someone who has the 'breath of life' in them. The word 'respiration' has to do with a person's regular breathing. *Inspire* is not mere breath, but rather it often has the connotation of sacred breath or infusion of something divine. The point of all this is that God breathed into or inspired the authors of Scripture."

"So did he just dictate it like they were secretaries or something?"

"The answer requires a distinction between the broad, general sense of Scripture's authorship and some narrow, particular examples. In a few specific examples, like the Ten Commandments, yes, God essentially inscribed his Word. But in the broad, general sense, God's inspiration of Scripture is a combination of divine and human authorship."

"What in the world does that mean?" asked Lauren. "I don't mean to be rude, but how can the Bible be divine and human? Doesn't it make sense that it is one or the other?"

MacGregor said, "There's definitely mystery surrounding how God inspired Scripture. Basically, we believe that the breath or Spirit of God superintended the efforts of the human authors. The human authors operated in the context of their historical situations, their personalities, their education and vocabularies, and vocations. And yet God's Spirit superintended the process to produce the Bible. We call it dual authorship. It's the mystery of the divine and human together producing Holy Scripture."

"What about all the contradictions and errors?"

"Can you show me any specific contradictions?" Brad challenged.

Lauren started to say something but then realized she didn't know of any. Had this conversation happened a month before, she would have let fly with her accusations of errors and faults about the Bible and Christianity, but she knew by now that anything she said would be severely tested. There was no point in throwing criticisms out there if she knew she couldn't back them up. "Well, no, that's a good point. I can't, not right now. Obviously I haven't read the Bible, so I can't think of anything specific. But, come on, this is *so* common. Most people just generally *know* that the Bible's got at least some problems."

MacGregor asked, "How do you think people come by this knowledge, especially so many people?"

"Well, I guess because a lot of people know the Bible has holes. Even the phrase I use—fairy tales and contradictions—is one I've heard lots of times."

MacGregor gently probed, "Do you think it's possible that maybe the idea of the Bible's problems has become part of popular culture and is transmitted without people actually questioning the idea? Perhaps that's why 'everyone knows,' and yet how many have actually even read it? Perhaps this widespread belief should itself be subjected to rigorous scrutiny by a skeptic."

"Yeah, I see what you're saying. But I just *feel,* again, like I believe or know something that I know most others believe, and you and Brad and Jarrod don't see it the way everybody else does."

"Maybe they have reasons for wanting the Bible to be wrong. Can you think of even one reason someone might *want* the Bible to be false?" asked the professor, leveling a steady gaze at Lauren's eyes.

Lauren looked down. As she had felt the first couple of weeks, the sense of MacGregor's having intuition about her life unnerved her. Yeah, she could think of a *huge* reason, but there was no way she could say that. Another awkward pause ensued, but Brad's impatience to press her on Scripture resumed the conversation.

"You've got a lot of passages in the Old Testament, especially the prophecy books, where it says, 'Thus says the Lord.' That's another internal claim that what follows is God's Word."

"What, you're not going to show me an actual verse?" Lauren teased.

Brad said, "I could, but there are literally hundreds of them, and the key part for my point is what I just said, 'Thus says the Lord.' If you really want to see them, we can start looking them up."

"No, that's OK. I'll take your word for it. So is that it? A few 'thus says the Lords' and the 'inspired' verse?"

"This is where I start to forget the points. I think there are one or two verses in Peter's letters that speak to this, but it's fuzzy. Is that right, Professor?"

"You are correct. Second Peter 1:20–21 is where you'll find one passage."

Brad located the verse and read, "'Above all, you must understand that no prophecy of Scripture came about by the prophet's own interpretation. For prophecy never had its origin in the will of man, but men spoke from God as they were carried along by the Holy Spirit.'"

"Wow," exclaimed Lauren with genuine surprise. "That's exactly what you were saying about the inspiration of the Spirit. What was your word?"

"Superintended."

"Yeah. This doesn't mean it's true, because I could write a letter and say that in speeches for communications class I was carried along by the Holy Spirit. But still I didn't realize that the Bible so clearly claimed to be God's Word. I thought that was just fundamentalist preacher talk."

"The other verse in Peter's letters that Brad meant is 2 Peter 3:15–16," suggested MacGregor. Brad took his cue and turned the page to read, "'Bear in mind that our Lord's patience means salvation, just as our dear brother Paul also wrote you with the wisdom that God gave him. He writes the same way in all his letters, speaking in them of these matters. His letters contain some things that are hard to understand, which ignorant and unstable people distort, as they do the other Scriptures, to their own destruction.'"

Brad expected Lauren to go ballistic about the "destruction" phrase, as she did at all mentions of judgment and wrath, but MacGregor quickly focused her attention. "You'll see that the key phrase for our purposes is that Peter refers to 'the rest of the Scriptures.' Thus, Paul's words are put on equal par with other Scriptures as being God's Word."

"OK, I get the point. You've got lots of verses that show the Bible's claim to be God's Word. But honestly, aren't there problems with the Bible even if I can't find them? I mean, if my religion professor was here, wouldn't he be able to show *some* problems? And what about mistakes in translations? And didn't the original words have to be copied over and over through the centuries? Even in a game of telephone, people make mistakes repeating a simple sentence, so surely there are at least some mistakes in copying the Bible."

"Sure, your professor might see problems. But remember, perhaps he is outside the story or wearing different lenses, and thus he's committed to other principles. He will not submit to Scripture and thus will try to distort it; he is not neutral. But, if I explained *how* the church community understands the Scriptures to be authoritative, I'm confident he would find our perspective at least tenable. The problem is that a lot of Christians, and sadly some who are quite public, hold to a naïve and substandard understanding of the Bible's authority. These uncritical, unreflective perspectives on Scripture's authority can and should be assailed by religion professors."

This made Brad nervous again, for it sounded as if the professor was taking sides with liberals against the ordinary Christian's trust in the Bible. "What is your sophisticated view of Scripture's authority?" asked Brad, a dollop of sarcasm seeping through.

As he usually did when challenged, MacGregor smiled. "Christian leaders in North America embarked on a project to hammer out our views of Scripture's authority in the face of attacks in the '60s and '70s.

"First, when we speak of Scripture as God's Word, we refer to the original manuscripts written by people like Luke or Paul. What Moses wrote, what David wrote in his psalms, what Peter wrote—that's the Word of God. You're right about the problems of copying and translation, but Christians affirm that our modern translations represent the Word of God to the extent that they faithfully represent the original manuscripts.

"I assure you, Lauren, as important as the Scriptures are to the church, enormous effort, time, and money have been spent for centuries to ensure our copies and translations are as accurate as possible. And we're confident that your Bible today essentially is faithful. Thus, we can be confident that the church essentially has God's Word. The Lord mysteriously superintended the finite, sinful human authors of Scripture, and we believe God has taken steps to ensure that what his church has today is essentially his Word."

"But isn't it just a lot of primitive writing about how the world came about?" asked Lauren. "We know so much more about how things really are today."

"Believing the Bible to be God's Word does not mean we demand the authors of Scripture conform to the standards of today. The group of orthodox scholars I talked about earlier produced some helpful statements that I accept. We say the Bible's authority is not diminished by a lack of scientific precision, occasional uncommon uses of grammar, rounding numbers, or hyperbole. Sometimes authors of Scripture arranged their material in nonchronological ways, which critics allege to prove that it's not God's Word. The writers had reasons for arranging their material the way they did, and we can't judge their work as nondivine simply because in our culture we would organize the material differently."

"As you say all that, it reminds me of a lot of things my religion professor said about the Bible and Christians. But you're saying that you agree with him?"

"No, I recognize that those elements are a part of Scripture. But to me, rounded numbers and ordinary observations of nature like 'the sun rising' are not proofs that the Bible is only a human document. Your professor probably listed these elements and said, 'God wouldn't author a book with these elements. Thus, the Bible is not God's Word.' What I'm saying is that Christians believe that Scripture is God's Word, and those elements are part of the dual authorship of God and humans. They are not blemishes on the fact of Scripture but rather interesting features of a document produced by a wonderfully mysterious partnership of God and people."

Lauren nodded. "I mean, that *sounds* plausible. It's at least a good defense against the charges. I still don't believe the Bible is actually God's Word, even though it claims to be. But I understand your position better."

"Good. The bottom line is that the Bible is God's special revelation to humanity. God showers us with information through general revelation, but people suppress that knowledge and worship created things instead. Therefore, God has given us special revelation in the form of the Word. If we study it and believe what it says, we enter into the Christian story. In the Scriptures we find out about the other example of special revelation."

"Which is? . . ." pressed Jarrod.

"Jesus himself. God reveals information about himself through his Son, Jesus. We'll get into this in a couple of weeks, I suspect. I won't explain it now, but I'll just say that Jesus is special revelation because he is the Word."

Everyone reflected quietly about this phrase, tired from a long week and a long evening of intense discussion. Jarrod picked up his magazines, as through to begin preparations for leaving, but stopped and asked, "So it's all about the story, huh? Where we go for the right information?"

"Yes, Jarrod, that's right. We all live by the stories of our community. That culture, in a sense, hands us a script as we grow up. The challenge is to let go of the scripts of the world and then enter into and live by the scripts of God. After all, that's why we call it *Scripture.*"

Chapter 10

Unfinished Business

THE ALARM BLARED in the crisp predawn morning, puncturing Brad's subconscious and dissipating the dream remnants in a dozen vapors. *Shoot,* he thought, *it is way, way too early for this.* His eyes, barely slit, found the digital clock, and he discovered that it really was too early. Then he remembered setting his clock the night before. *Oh yeah. Shoot.*

As the outlines of the idea came back to his mind, a little motivation began to drip into his spirit. The professor had pulled him aside and inquired how Brad might reconnect with God. Brad suggested that he try waking up twenty minutes earlier and spending some time reading the Bible and praying, things he had done most days throughout his life until he graduated from college and started working. These days it was sporadic. No, who was he kidding, he thought, as he rolled out of bed, sporadic was before business school. These days it was almost never.

First stop, coffeemaker. Jarrod, ever and effortlessly on the cutting edge, had told him about Pura Vida coffee, and Brad ordered a bag from their Web site. Best coffee purchase he had ever made. They sold terrific pouches of the java bean from Costa Rica and Guatemala, and they ensnared Brad with their "local flavor" roasting process. The sweet smell, restive percolation, and steam began to revive him, even before a drop passed his lips. *I'm just like Pavlov's dog,* he mused.

A trip to the bathroom, mug in hand, led to splashing some cold water on his face, after which Brad yawned and stumbled his way back to the bedroom. He seriously contemplated falling back into bed and snagging the lost twenty minutes back before getting ready for work. "I don't get enough sleep to do this in the morning." A huge yawn overtook him.

Brad had to paw around his bookcase, pushing various books around until he found his Bible. The bed beckoned mightily, but lessons from his junior high youth pastor came back even in this fog. Brad plopped instead on a stuffed chair, spilling a bit of coffee on his T-shirt, and the heat stinging his skin woke him up a bit more. He gruffly turned pages, hunting for what MacGregor had suggested. Brad wanted to start back with Paul's letters, but MacGregor said something to Brad about him "getting romanced by God" in the Psalms. Brad was fairly sure he had never heard such a term applied to God in all his life, but he knew he didn't have a lot of ground to stand on.

Brad took another sip as his left hand found Psalm 1. He read:

> Blessed is the man
>   who does not walk in the counsel of the wicked
>   or stand in the way of sinners
>   or sit in the seat of mockers.
> But his delight is in the law of the LORD,
>   and on his law he meditates day and night.
> He is like a tree planted by streams of water,
>   which yields its fruit in season
>   and whose leaf does not wither.
> Whatever he does prospers.

The old, familiar words came back to him. He could hear the preacher at Inwood Drive Baptist in his memory, walking the congregation through the words "follow," "take," and "sit." He thought of a recent after-hours get-together with the other Richmond Steinberg associates where he had given in to temptation to make fun of some service industry folks. He knew better than to call attention to those less fortunate, let alone laugh at them. *Jarrod is right about me,* he realized. *I've become a callous jerk.*

He read verse 2 again: *"His delight is in the law of the Lord, and on his law he meditates day and night."* Memories of being thrilled by getting to know God better when he was in high school came back.

Being planted. Yielding fruit. Prospering. Brad read those words, and his heart yearned for them. He loved the challenge of banking, but he was tired of being blown around in his schedule, keeping crazy hours. He was already tired of the travel. He wanted more responsibility. That would be yielding fruit. Prospering—he was doing this one, but he knew he could be let go any time because of the economic downturn.

Brad exhaled. He scanned the rest of the psalm. He wanted these things, and he wanted not to be on the path of wickedness. This was it. So simple. His eyes drooped, not from fatigue this time, but from the realization that he needed the Lord again. And finally, for the first time in weeks and weeks, Brad prayed outside of a church service.

† † †

Lauren's office at B&K hummed more quietly than usual as even fewer deals were in the pipeline. Things weren't dead, but they weren't fast. Annette picked a good time to call.

"Hey! Thanks for calling, Annette," said Lauren. "I'm sorry I have not called back about how my life is going. I've actually been somewhat better."

"Really?"

"Well, sort of. At least I've been distracted a lot when I'm not at work. This professor has been spending time with Jarrod, Brad, and me."

"Well, what did Dr. Ffeir say? Wasn't he amazing?"

"I don't know, Annette. We got off on the wrong foot, and I had to be a bit firm with him. He actually took it well, and I was able to explain more what's going on with me."

"Oh, Lauren, tell me you didn't do all the talking."

"Well, why not? He was off chasing these tangents and then just repeating everything back to me. It was a waste of time."

"Lauren, you know *we* do this with egotistical clients. How many times have we joked about this? They feel a need to assert themselves, and we put our feet up on the desk and let the meter run. I'm surprised you let that happen to you."

"Things got a lot better after I took control, Annette. And I went back for another session."

"Well, has he helped you?"

"I don't know. I think I've been so distracted outside of work, as I said, that I've not had a lot of time to think. I mean, no, the sense of something wrong rumbling around inside me is still there, but I've not had those moments when I feel so terribly empty."

"Hmm, I don't know what to say. I want to support you whatever you do."

"Thanks, Annette. You know I appreciate your helping like this. I'm going to see Dr. Ffeir again. I know I'm not through this."

"OK. Keep me posted. And let's go out dancing this weekend. Do you have plans Friday?"

† † †

Jarrod buzzed Brad. "Dude, how's life?"

"Hey, man. Things are good. Not too crazy here right now, though I'll probably be here till eight or nine tonight. How are you?"

"I'm really good. Just stepped out of the library to take a break from reading. I'm in some deep waters, Brad. It's exciting stuff in some ways, but this is so much harder than undergrad. I'm struggling to keep up."

"You'll do fine. You always do."

"I don't know. It's a lot harder. I'm realizing that all the philosophy I did at UT was a totally different kind. The courses I took in Austin were traditional philosophy. At Rice they're into this Continental philosophy, and it's hard for me to get my mind around it. Frankly, I can't believe they let me in the program."

"If they'd known you were such a religious weirdo, they probably wouldn't have." Brad knew Jarrod smiled at this. "But Jarrod, don't all grad students say they can't believe they got in?"

"Yeah, that's true, except for business school students."

"Good point."

"But, Brad, here's why I called: my reading today is a lot like what Professor MacGregor was talking about down in Galveston. It's new to me, but it's starting to make a little sense."

"That's great, Jarrod. And you know, that brings up something I haven't mentioned in a long time—"

"The whole integration thing?"

"Yeah. What do you say? Maybe your bottom-line business friend has a point this time?"

"No, I think you're right. That's why I was smiling as I read this chapter this morning. I thought of MacGregor, and I thought of how you used to push me to put my faith and my intellectual interests together. Today it's making sense."

"You mean you're not afraid of ending up all cognitive and dead in your faith?"

"No, I am! But hanging out with the professor and this recent reading is making me see that I've got to pull my life together somehow."

"Jarrod, this is good. I'm glad you think so. It's ironic that you bring this up because I've not been reading my Bible much at all in the last couple of years. MacGregor challenged me a bit, so this morning I got up and read. It was amazing. I think if you start studying Scripture, you're going to love it."

"Dude, you make it sound like I'm anti-Bible. You know I respect it."

"I know, I know. Believe me, I remember. But maybe we can do the same thing together. Today I started reading it again, and you can do this with me. And we can talk about it. And as we meet with MacGregor, you can work on integrating your intellectual world with your faith."

"Deal. And you will work on integrating this stuff with your world."

"Deal. Thanks, Jarrod. I know you ride me hard sometimes, but today I'm on cloud nine from reading Psalm 1 this morning. MacGregor was right; I have missed God. Today it's amazing what a difference it makes at work."

"Really? How so?"

"I just feel at peace. The swirl still happens around me, but I'm at peace today. Any irritation I felt toward folks here is just gone. At least for now. I feel Christ living through me today. It's like old times. This is great."

"Good deal. I'm glad."

"But I've got to get back to work. You want to get together at Common Grounds tonight?"

"With Lauren?"

"Sure. I'll call her."

"You're on. Have a great rest of the day. See you around 9:30?"

"Yep. Go philosophize."

† † †

They sat at one of the outside tables. The weather cooperated beautifully—crisp sixty-five degree weather and the smell of incipient fall. Lauren and Brad arrived together, still wearing their business clothes, and Jarrod showed up in his jeans, sandals, and azure alpaca V-necked sweater shirt. Lauren smiled when she saw him. She had two friends who were utterly good-looking and in completely different ways.

Jarrod told Lauren about what he and Brad had decided, but she just looked on noncommittally. "What, you don't want us getting excited about this?" Jarrod asked.

"No, that's fine. But you can't expect me to get excited about you two getting more interested in something that I don't share and actually disagree with."

"I thought you enjoyed the time we've spent with the professor," said Brad.

"I have. It's been interesting—you know, intellectually stimulating. He's definitely made me think, and I'll even admit he's changed my thinking in some small ways."

"Like what?" asked Jarrod.

"Well, like about tolerance. And realizing that I don't feel awe for God the way you do. It's made me wonder if I'm missing something about God. Not that I think you are right or that I believe in the God of the Bible. I don't. But I'm feeling uneasy or that something's missing about my spirituality."

"You don't want to join Jarrod and me in reading the Bible and talking to MacGregor about it?" inquired Brad.

"Brad, please. I'm not that stupid. You think I'll fall for something that easily? I know, deep in the back of your mind, that you're always trying to convert me. I hardly want to join your project just so you can harangue me about going to hell."

"Lauren, come on. Have I ever said anything like that?"

She waited a while before answering with a grin. "Well, not in the last five or six years, I suppose. But you still think it. I know you."

Jarrod intervened. "Look, forget the Bible reading. I'd rather just do it with Brad anyway. But I do want to keep hanging out with Professor MacGregor. Spending time with him has been amazingly cool."

"Definitely," said Brad.

"I don't know. I feel like I'm learning a lot about your Christian world, even though we've been friends forever. And he's sweet. And it is actually fun. But I just feel this thing inside pulling me away. Like I know this is bad and weird for me to be around."

"Do you mind if he keeps coming here on Sunday nights?" asked Jarrod.

"No, I guess not. I guess I just look forward to when we're done with this phase and we can just get back to normal. You know, with just us."

"I was going to call him and see if we can meet next Sunday, after this one."

Lauren sighed. "Yeah. Let's do it."

† † †

Jarrod got a call on his mobile and eased out to meet a female grad student for a study session. The smile on his face told Brad that she must be bright and cute, and Brad smiled back. Lauren pretended not to notice but said good-bye.

After Jarrod left, Brad put a new question to her. "Lauren, I don't get it. You've been different. Are you just wiped out from work?"

"No, I don't know. I have been more tired. And irritable. I don't know."

"Are you still mad at me?"

"No. I told you everything is fine."

"Yes, you did. But it wasn't fine."

Lauren didn't respond.

"Look, I'm really sorry."

"Brad, you don't have to apologize. I told you, it's fine. I'm not mad anymore."

"So you're OK with the whole not dating non-Christians thing?"

"It's funny you mention it. I've actually been thinking a lot about this since our time in Galveston. I'm really realizing how different you and MacGregor are, and in his own way, Jarrod. You really see the world differently. Most of the time we've been friends I thought we were basically the same, but you had this wacko, extremist part of you that didn't fit with the rest of you, and as long as you didn't trot it out in public, things were fine. But now I'm getting how different you are."

"We do see the world differently."

"I guess for the first time it makes sense. I mean, when Professor MacGregor was asking me those questions about being married to one of the religious extremists from Louisiana, I got his point. It made sense then, but I didn't like it. For some reason, now I get it. I really understand why you and I shouldn't date."

They looked at each other for a long time, without a trace of romantic longing, just the deep understanding of good friends.

"Let's go," said Brad.

As they walked out, Brad put his arm around her and pulled her close.

Discussion Questions

Chapter 1: *A DANGEROUS KISS*
and Chapter 2: *COFFEE MATTERS*

Whom do you relate to in this story? (Brad, Lauren, Jarrod, MacGregor) Why do you connect with this character the most? Read Romans 8:28; Psalm 139:16; Proverbs 16:9; Acts 4:27.

When do you feel like life is meaningless?

What gives you joy in life?

Chapter 3: *GOD IN HITLER*

Do you ever feel weird talking about religion with others? Why or why not?

How would you describe God?

When you say "God is righteous," what does that mean?

Where do you get your information about God?

How would you respond to Lauren's belief that the Bible is an ancient book of myths and contradictions?

Chapter 4: *THE GRAND CANYON*

Read John 14:6. What does that verse tell you about Jesus?

God is omnipresent. Reflect on Psalm 139 and express your thoughts and feelings about this concept.

How does the majestic power of an all-knowing, everywhere-present God make you feel? Lauren says it frightens her. How about you?

Discuss the quote from *The Lion, the Witch and the Wardrobe:* "Safe? No, he's not safe; he's a lion. But he's good."

Does the God you worship inspire awe? Why or why not?

Chapter 5: *GOD'S SCHEDULE* and Chapter 6: *9/11 AND GOD'S SCHEDULE*

Do you believe God has a schedule? How does that make you feel?

Read Ephesians 1:11; Job 37:6–13. If God is in control, "he rules and reigns," then how can our choices have real meaning?

Do you ever have trouble trusting the Father's will? Why or why not?

Is the God you are "coming to know" full of grace and truth? How has he shown you his grace?

How much do you long for God? Are you spending time with God on a daily basis? If not, do you miss him? Read Psalm 34:8; Isaiah 46:9–10.

Just how big is your God? Is your God adequate to the task of "being God"?

MacGregor says that Brad does not pray because he does not believe it works. Does prayer really work? Why or why not?

Lauren says God seems remote sometimes. How do you relate to her feelings?

Read Matthew 10:29–31. Do you feel God's incredible love for you in these verses? How valuable are you in the Father's eyes?

Why is mystery so hard to grasp?

What does the cross tell us about pain and suffering?

How did you feel after 9/11? How did your view of God change after that day?

Chapter 7: *CREATION SPEAKS*

How would you respond to this question from a skeptic: What about the person who has never heard about God? What will happen to him?

Read Romans 1:18–25. What does this passage teach you about "the person who has never heard"?

In light of Psalm 19:1–4, how does nature reveal the character of God?

Why is intolerance such a touchy subject in our society today?

Where does Lauren's "tolerance philosophy" break down?

What is God's standard for people? Support your answer with Scripture.

How does Jarrod define *pluralism?* What are some problems inherent in this worldview?

Discuss John Calvin's term, the *sensus divinitatis.* What does it mean to "suppress the light"?

Chapter 8: VOGUE *AND THE* WALL STREET JOURNAL and Chapter 9: *STORIES WE LIVE BY*

What is special revelation? How is it different from general revelation?

Who are some authorities or experts you look to? What sets their advice over all the rest?

Why are all authorities, religious or secular, biased?

Do you believe it is possible to be neutral? Explain your answer.

How does everyone "reason in a circle" to some extent?

Read 2 Timothy 3:16. Why is this verse crucial to the Christian faith?

What are two examples of special revelation? How do they relate to each other?

Discuss some major turning points in your life.

Contrast "the world's story" with "the Christian story."

How have you responded to God's special revelation of Jesus Christ? Do you know him personally or would you say that you are still seeking?

About the Authors

BEN YOUNG, M.DIV., author and speaker, is the associate pastor of worship at Second Baptist Church in Houston, Texas. He is a graduate of Southwestern Baptist Theological Seminary and Baylor University, and the coauthor of three other books. Ben also leads seminars throughout the country on how to build successful dating relationships. He hosted *The Single Connection,* a nationally syndicated radio talk show just for singles, and directed one of the country's largest singles' ministries at the 30,000-member Second Baptist Church in Houston. Ben and Dr. Sam Adams recently coauthored three books on relationships, *The Ten Commandments of Dating, The One: A Realistic Guide to Choosing a Soul Mate,* and *Devotions for Dating Couples.*

GLENN LUCKE graduated from Dartmouth College and Reformed Theological Seminary (M.Div.) and is currently pursuing his doctorate at the University of Virginia. He served as a campus minister at Harvard University, writes numerous booklets and devotional guides, and speaks at regional and national conferences.

Glenn is working with Caedmon's Call to launch *Christ & Culture,* an annual conference that equips and motivates believers to engage and impact culture, inspiring them to create culture that glorifies Christ. He started Docent Communications Group, which creates customized sermon research for pastors and communicators. For more information, please visit www.docentgroup.com.